Social Work in Primary Care

SAGE SOURCEBOOKS FOR THE HUMAN SERVICES SERIES

Series Editors: ARMAND LAUFFER and CHARLES GARVIN

A source is a starting point, a place of origin, information, or payoff. The volumes in this series reflect these themes. For readers they will serve as starting points for new programs, as the place of origin of advanced skills, or as a source for information that can be used in the pursuit of professional and organizational goals.

Sage Sourcebooks are written to provide multiple benefits for both professionals and advanced students. Authors and contributors are recognized authorities in their fields or at the cutting edge of new knowledge and technique. Sourcebooks deal with new and emerging practice tools and current and anticipated policy issues, transforming knowledge from allied professions and the social sciences into information applicable to the human services.

Matthew L. Henk
editor

Social Work in Primary Care

SAGE SOURCEBOOKS FOR THE HUMAN SERVICES SERIES   8

SAGE PUBLICATIONS
The Publishers of Professional Social Science
Newbury Park   London   New Delhi

For information address:

SAGE Publications, Inc.
2111 West Hillcrest Drive
Newbury Park, California 91320

SAGE Publications Ltd.
28 Banner Street
London EC1Y 8QE
England

SAGE Publications India Pvt. Ltd.
M-32 Market
Greater Kailash I
New Delhi 110 048 India

Printed in the United States of America

Library of Congress Cataloging-in-Publications Data

Main entry under title:

Social work in primary care / edited by Matthew L. Henk.
        p.   cm. — (Sage sourcebooks for the human services series ;
8)
        Bibliography: p.
        ISBN 0–8039–3035–6. — ISBN 9–8039–3036–4 (pbk.)
        1. Medical social work—United States.   I. Henk, Matthew L.
II. Series: Sage sourcebooks for the human services series ; v. 8.
HV687.5.U5S6447   1989
362.1'0425—dc20   89–10237
                                                            CIP

FIRST PRINTING, 1989

CONTENTS

ACKNOWLEDGMENTS

I would like to express my gratitude to Paul Fischer, Chris Siefert, Juanita Evans, and Betty Rusnack for their encouragement; Charles Garvin and Sage Publications for their interest and advice; the authors and reviewers for their time, effort, and expertise; the Public Health Service and The University of Rochester Family Medicine Residency Program for their cooperation; and Julie Tenenbaum and Barbara Royster for their editing assistance.

PREFACE

This volume is intended to prepare social work students and practitioners to function in primary care settings. During the last 15 years "primary care" has emerged as a dominant force in American medicine. Improvements in the health status of patients will no longer occur as a result of technology and specialized treatments, but rather as a result of early detection and treatment of diseases; the development of health promotion and disease prevention programs; and the treatment of psychosocial problems. Social workers have an important and pivotal role in these efforts. Although physicians and other medical staff need to become involved in the development of prevention programs and in the solution of psychosocial problems, they do not always have the time or ability to do so.

Ultimately society will need to address each existing or potential patient problem if it intends to have a healthy populace and to reduce costs. One need not look any further than the AIDS epidemic to understand the emotional, physical and financial costs that occur when needed prevention services are not provided. Problems left unattended do not disappear. They only become more acute, complex, and costly to treat.

The primary care setting is fertile ground for the development of a variety of social work practices. Each role or type of practice needs to be clearly understood when the social worker negotiates a position within a primary care setting. (Although each role is distinct, the problem-solving process provides a common thread.) The rapid growth of primary care practices will provide employment opportunities only if social work professionals can understand and adapt to such settings. Since social work graduate schools' didactic curriculum and field placements are not oriented to this type of practice setting, it is essential that some basic concepts be provided to those who might choose this type of career opportunity. The following text attempts to provide some of these concepts.

Primary care practices are unique service settings insofar as they allow the practitioners to initiate interventions prior to the patients' requesting the service. Such practices also can track and monitor the progress of health care plans to ensure that compliance is accomplished.

The contract between the patient and the setting clearly dictates that the setting has a major responsibility to preserve and improve the health of its enrolled patients. This does not exempt the patients from taking responsibility for their own health, but requires the setting and its staff to make every effort to ensure the patients receive those services that are needed to solve their problems.

Social work professionals have the necessary problem-solving skills to meet the needs of the primary care setting and the patients they serve. The contents of this book will provide: a historical perspective of social work in health care and in primary care; a justification for interdisciplinary collaboration; a model for the integration of social work into the educational setting; a description of the variety of roles social workers can play; and some insight regarding the physician's and administrator's views of the need for social work services in primary care.

INTRODUCTION

"We should not be oppressed by the system but rather use systems for human progress" (Campbell, 1988). Primary care is one component of a large, complex, and potentially intimidating medical care system, yet it holds unlimited potential to improve the quality of human life. During the past 15 years primary health care has emerged as a dominant force in modern medicine. It has become apparent that major improvements in the patients' health status no longer will occur as a result of new technologies, medications, or more specialized treatment, but rather as a result of early detection and treatment of disease, the development of health promotion, disease prevention programs, and early treatment of psychosocial problems. Social work has a pivotal role to play in these efforts. If social workers are to integrate successfully into primary care settings, we need to understand the goals and values of primary care. More important, however, we must have a clear idea of the roles, functions, and tasks we could perform in this type of setting. Consequently, much of this text focuses on role definitions.

The text also provides information on the history of social work in health care and primary care, interprofessional collaboration, a model for integration of social work in the educational setting, the physician's and administrator's perspectives, record keeping and data management, and future trends.

DEFINING PRIMARY CARE

Primary care is defined in a variety of ways by various authors. Common denominators include:

The setting and its providers are contacted first when the patient needs health and psychosocial services.

Care, when it is provided, is comprehensive and continuous: comprehensive insofar as the providers identify and treat most biological and psychosocial problems on site, and continuous insofar as the providers assume responsibility to ensure hospital and other specialized services are appropriate and timely.

What is not often stated but essential to the concept of primary care is a unique but implicit contract between the patient and the setting. This contract dictates that the setting will assume major responsibility both to preserve and improve the health of enrolled patients. Not since the settlement house movement has a service institution assumed such responsibilities for a specific target population across such a wide range of problem areas be they biological, personal, familial, or environmental. This relationship also allows the primary care setting to initiate interventions before the patient requests a service and to track the progress of individual health plans to ensure compliance.

The following are examples of how other authors define primary care. The American Academy of Family Practice (AAFP) adopted the following definition of primary care in October 1975:

> Primary Care is a type of medical care delivery which emphasizes first contact care and assumes on-going responsibility for the patient in both health maintenance and therapy of illness. It is personal care involving unique interaction and communication between the patient and physician. It is comprehensive in scope and includes an overall coordination of care of the patient's health problems; be they biological, behavioral, or social, the appropriate use of consultants in community resources is an important part of effective primary care. (*AAFP Official Definition*, 1975)

Dr. John Renner states that: "Primary Care can best be understood in the context of 14 measurable components." These components include:

1. Screening
2. Preventive medicine
3. Health care assessment
4. Self-care, including both patient education and patient participation
5. Episodic care
6. Continuous care including chronic care
7. Team delivery as opposed to single physician care
8. Referral and consultation
9. Family and community relationships
10. Social and physiological factors
11. Personal care
12. Office management including efficiency of office operations

13. The ability to adapt and to accent dynamic change in the health care field

14. System-oriented care including knowledge of access distribution and quality control in cost effectiveness. (Renner, 1977)

At a philosophical level, primary care seeks to put into operation basic principles of social justice, equality, and individual responsibility for health. In this context, primary care encompasses diverse activities and concepts ranging from efforts to enhance accessibility of care and legislative reforms, to recognition of the role of other sectors of the society — housing, employment, education — in health and illness. As a set of activities, primary care focuses on treatment of common diseases and health education, including prevention. In this context, attention to psychosocial components of illness is an intrinsic component of primary care. (Schlesinger, 1985)

What is apparent in these definitions is the compatibility and similarity between the philosophy and values of primary care and those of social work. Just as the primary care specialty of family practice endeavors to treat patients comprehensively with health care being the first priority, social work attempts to solve each problem affecting the client beginning with psychosocial issues. In reality both professionals must attempt to determine which problems are most significant and develop a plan to intervene with each problem according to priority. Although our values are similar, patient ownership issues can present problems, particularly in those primary care settings in which the employer is not an institution such as a health maintenance organization (HMO), hospital or community health center, but rather a private for-profit practice. Such issues will be discussed in the chapter on interprofessional collaboration.

PRIMARY CARE SETTINGS

Primary care can be provided by a variety of settings if the premise and criteria previously described are accepted. Each setting must be clearly understood if social workers are to negotiate an appropriate role. These settings include:

1. Federally sponsored Community Health Centers and Migrant Health Centers funded under Public Law 95:63, Section 330 and 329. These programs are designed to serve urban, rural, and migrant communities

that are medically underserved and critically short of physicians. The goals are to provide not only medical services but also health promotion, mental health, nutrition, pharmaceutical, and dental services.

2. Health maintenance organizations that are both privately and federally funded.

3. Group practices that are either multispecialty or family practice and solo practices of family physicians, internists, and pediatricians.

4. Ambulatory or outpatient clinics of private, public, and university hospitals.

5. State, county, and city maternity and infant care, children and youth care, and primary care projects.

6. Family medicine residency programs sponsored by hospitals or universities. Generally, services are provided by family practice residents and faculty.

Many health care programs identify themselves as "primary care centers" because the term has such a positive connotation. Unfortunately, many of these settings are unable to meet the criteria established by the previous authors or organizations. Some physician groups, HMOs, community health centers, and hospital outpatient services are unwilling or unable to provide the comprehensive and continuous care that patients need. Although they may provide acute, episodic, first-encounter care, they do not accept the responsibility to maintain and improve the health status of enrolled patients. Health promotion/disease prevention programs and other comprehensive services are nonexistent or minimal at best in many of these so-called primary care settings.

If a patient is male, over 40, with a family history of heart disease and has not been screened for cholesterol; if the patient is over 65 or has significant heart or lung problems and has not been offered a flu shot; if the patient sees a different physician on each visit; if the patient has a significant psychosocial problem that has gone undetected or untreated, then the patient probably is not enrolled in an ideal primary care setting. To accomplish the ideal requires physicians that will accept and implement primary care concepts, an administration that will support these concepts, and a multidisciplined team of providers to meet patient needs.

WHAT IS THE SOCIAL WORKER'S ROLE?

The essence of this book is to provide a clear picture of the various roles, functions, and tasks for social workers in the primary care setting. Primary care organizations have struggled with the decision to develop a multispecialty group practice model consisting of pediatric, internal medicine, and obstetric physicians or a family practice model using family physicians, physicians' assistants, and nurse clinicians. Administrators and physicians struggle also to decide if the social worker should function as a generalist or specialist. Conceptually, the generalist is the easier role to understand because theoretically this role can meet most of the needs of the patients and the institution. Also, the role is more desirable because it is diverse and uses all the social worker's skills and knowledge. In reality, however, one generalist social worker cannot meet all the patient needs of most primary care practices. Three physicians usually see 4500 patients and have 12,600 patient encounters each year. If the ideal system is to be achieved — which requires that all existing and potential problems be addressed — then more than one social worker is needed. Because the ideal and the real rarely meet, priorities will have to be set and ultimately some patient needs will not be met. Because each setting has unique needs based on patient problems, institutional demands, funding requirements, and economic necessities, the social worker must carefully analyze the setting's expectations and patient needs before committing to a specific role.

Some examples of how roles are developed include:

1. *Demand*
   A federally funded community health center receives a supplemental grant to provide case management services for perinatal patients.
   Likely Response
   Hire social worker in an advocacy/brokerage role.

2. *Demand*
   A private for-profit group of physicians would like to manage more of their own patients with psychosocial problems.
   Likely Response
   Hire a social work consultant part-time to provide necessary training and consultation.

3. *Demand*
   An HMO that has many middle-class patients with family problems and little need for advocacy with community agencies.
   Likely Response
   Hire a social worker in a therapist or mental health role.

4. *Demand*
   A for-profit group associated with a university hospital needs to meet the
   emotional and family problems of its patients but is unable to pay the full
   salary for a social worker.
   Likely Response
   Hire a social worker in therapist role who can bill paying patients for
   counseling services.

Role clarification is essential if social work services are to be an
integral component of the primary care setting. Social workers must be
clear about the services we can provide for each type of primary care
setting. With over 6,000 hospitals, 800 Community Health Centers and
Maternal and Child Health Programs, 350 family practice residency
programs, 1,000 HMOs, countless for-profit group practices, and
industry moving into the provision of primary care for its employees,
social work needs to capitalize on this unique opportunity.

The information provided in the text will help social workers integrate smoothly into the primary care setting. This integration will
improve the scope and quality of care for the patient, provide a meaningful role for the social worker, assist the physician in the management of psychosocial problems, and demonstrate that primary care
settings are truly committed to provide comprehensive care for all their
patients.

REFERENCES

AAFP Official Definition of Primary Care. (1975). Kansas City, MO: AAFP Reprint 302.
Campbell, Joseph. (1988). *The power of myth* [Series with Bill Moyers]. PBS TV. New
    York: Doubleday.
Renner, John. (1977). Academic missions of family medicine. In T. E. Bryan (Ed.),
    Fogarty International Center proceedings. Washington, DC: DHEW Publications
    No. (NIH) 77-1062.
Schlesinger, E. G. (1985). *Health care social work practice: Concepts and strategies.*
    St. Louis: Times Mirror/Mosby.

Chapter 1

HISTORICAL DEVELOPMENT OF SOCIAL WORK IN PRIMARY CARE

Louise Doss-Martin
Deborah J. Stokes

George Santayana has written, "Those who cannot remember the past are condemned to repeat it." This chapter reviews historical developments so we can more fully understand the present and prepare for the future. It includes:

- a brief summary of major developments in the United States' health care delivery system and the predominant health problems in this country
- a review of milestones in the evolution of social work in health care, with emphasis on primary care
- a review of social work efforts to provide better continuing education and research regarding primary care issues
- the results of a recent study of social work services in primary care settings in the midwest.

MAJOR DEVELOPMENTS IN THE HEALTH CARE SYSTEM FROM 1850 TO PRESENT

The period between 1850 and 1900 saw the development of large hospitals (such as Bellevue in New York and Massachusetts General

NOTE: This chapter was prepared by government employees as part of their official duties; therefore, the material is in the public domain and may be reproduced or copied without permission.

Hospital in Boston), symbolizing the earliest institutionalization of health care in the United States. Before 1850, health care in this country was an unorganized collection of individual services operating autonomously and independently of each other. From 1900 to 1940, the scientific method was introduced into United States medicine. The opening of Johns Hopkins University Medical School in Baltimore began the development of a solid scientific base from which medicine would be transformed from an informal collection of "generalities and good intentions" into a detailed and clearly defined science.

With the advent of World War II, the United States experienced major social, technological, and political changes. These changes were marked by:

1. an intense interest in the social and organizational structure of the health care delivery system
2. a review of the financing of health insurance plans such as Blue Cross/ Blue Shield
3. an increasing concentration of power in the federal government exemplified by the passage of the Hospital Survey and Construction Act (Hill-Burton Act) and the funding of large research institutes such as the National Institutes of Health
4. the passage of Medicare and Medicaid legislation
5. a change in philosophy suggesting that health care is a right, not a privilege.

Since 1980 health care programs such as hospitals, nursing homes, and ambulatory care facilities began to move toward privatization, which reemphasized cost effectiveness and cost containment. Methods of financing and delivering care were also reorganized (Torrens, 1984).

Numerous other changes have moved health care delivery from hospitals into primary care settings. Examples include changes in financing, health care technology, and settings, along with changes in life-styles, values, and education of the physician. Health care and hospitals were once synonymous, because most patients did not seek health care until the latter stages of disease. Health promotion and disease prevention are recent phenomena.

New technologies such as X-ray, laboratory, and other diagnostic equipment allowed the primary care physicians to diagnose and treat patients in their offices. They no longer needed to refer patients to subspecialists or to the hospitals. New equipment, more compact and easier to use, enabled primary care physicians to manage more patients for longer periods of time. This enabled primary care physicians to capture a greater market share of patients and ensured the viability of their practices.

To purchase this new equipment, provide more effective management of the business, and allow time off for vacations and continuing education, primary care physicians had to develop larger and more complex systems of care such as group practices, health maintenance organizations (HMOs), community health centers, and hospital outpatient departments. The solo practice was no longer the practice of choice. The establishment of these large systems created a new demand for social work services because the patients' psychosocial and lifestyle problems could be more effectively addressed.

PREDOMINANT HEALTH PROBLEMS IN THE UNITED STATES: PAST AND PRESENT

Most social workers in practice today do not have a firsthand understanding of or appreciation for the devastating role that epidemics played in the lives of Americans in the eighteenth and nineteenth centuries. Plague, cholera, typhoid, influenza, pneumonia, yellow fever and a host of other diseases were widespread. These diseases related primarily to impure food, contaminated water supply, inadequate sewage disposal, and poor hygiene and housing conditions.

By 1900, increases in the number of health departments and the improvements in environmental conditions — including improved systems for water purification, sanitary disposal of sewage, and safeguards regarding the quality of milk and food — led to the elimination of many epidemics that had plagued humanity for centuries.

The arrival of the antibiotic era in the 1940s revolutionized effective treatment for infectious disease. In effect, prior to the advent of Acquired Immune Deficiency Syndome (AIDS), antibodic therapies had successfully eradicated deaths from infectious disease. However, the AIDS epidemic, characterized as the "new plague" by some, poses an ominous threat to the lives of increasing millions of persons worldwide; such as, it presents a major challenge to public health resources and primary care systems. Having recognized this notable exception, it is still true that, by and large, antibiotics brought the era of death by infectious disease to a close and allowed people to live longer. Unfortunately, people also developed long-term chronic illnesses such as heart disease, cancer, and stroke, which now account for two-thirds of all deaths. Because these chronic illnesses or new morbidities are related to personal life-styles and the environment, social work will have an important role in preventing disease and providing services to those already ill. Two other conditions, anxiety and depression, are often in the top 10 most diagnosed problems in primary care settings, and these problems cannot be addressed by physicians alone (see Chapter 4).

While these chronic illnesses have become the major cause of death and disability since the 1950s, organized health services have not kept pace with this new set of circumstances:

> Unfortunately, the organization of our health services is still modeled on the disease patterns that were predominant in the 1900-1945 period and concentrates on individual episodes as if they were separate and distinct entities. As a result, the health care system is primarily short term and discontinuous in nature, and it treats chronic illness as if it were merely a series of acute episodes. This trend is further reinforced by the current method of financing of health services, with its great emphasis on paying for individual services rendered rather than on the long-term, continuous nature of the underlying disease process. (Torrens, 1984)

The new morbidities challenge us to establish systems of care that are more continuous, comprehensive, and preventive. In this regard, social workers can make many contributions:

1. Using a full network of community resources to marshal a wide range of services on behalf of the patient and family, which the primary care program alone is unable to provide.
2. Educating the whole family to minimize isolation of the identified patient and to support family members in their respective roles, despite the presence/interference of a chronic illness or disability.
3. Developing interventions for the individuals and community to improve or maintain the patient's health.
4. Advising and consulting with other health care providers so they can better serve their patients.
5. Providing mental health services to the patient.

HISTORICAL DEVELOPMENT OF SOCIAL WORK IN PRIMARY CARE

Massachusetts General Hospital with the assistance of Dr. Richard C. Cabot initiated one of the first departments in medical social work in 1905. Dr. Cabot recognized that a patient's social situation affects the results of treatment. The intention of what was then a new concept in medical care was to treat the patient as an individual to help him make more effective use of what the physician and the hospital had to offer (National Association of Social Workers, 1971). At that time, social work services were confined primarily to hospitalized patients and those attending outpatient clinics.

The years of 1916 and 1918 marked the beginning of the utilization of social workers in specialty clinics offered by public authorities such as baby clinics and the Municipal Child Welfare Centers. During this same period, a historical event was taking place that would chart the course for public health social work practice in primary care settings. On April 9, 1912, the bill establishing a Children's Bureau was signed into law. Its purpose was to "investigate and report upon all matters pertaining to the welfare of children and child life among all classes of our people." The bill focused on investigating "infant mortality, the birth rate, orphanages, juvenile courts, desertion, dangerous occupations, accidents and diseases of children, employment, legislation affecting children in the several States and Territories" (Bradbury, 1962).

Four of the first five chiefs of the Children's Bureau were social workers: Julia Lathrop (1912-1921); Grace Abbott (1921-1934); Katherine F. Linroot (1935-1951); and Katherine Oettinger (1957-1962). The fourth chief, Martha May Eliot, a physician, had worked briefly in the social service department at Massachusetts General Hospital before entering medical school (Evans, 1983).

During the formative years of the Children's Bureau, social workers actively investigated and reported on issues relating to the welfare of children. Studies of infant and maternal mortality called attention not only to the socioeconomic factors underlying high infant and maternal mortality rates but also the number of preventable prenatal conditions involved (O'Hara, 1978).

Realizing that all of the gains for these vulnerable populations could diminish without a formal legislative mandate, the social workers of the Children's Bureau led a campaign that resulted in passage of the Sheppard-Towner Act of 1921. The work accomplished under this Act contributed substantially to the reduction of infant mortality in the United States, demonstrated the effectiveness of such preventive health services, and established the principle of shared federal-state responsibility in matters of health and social welfare. While today we fully accept the appropriate role of the federal and state governments to provide major funding, to set standards and to lead in establishing and providing primary care services, at that time such a notion was considered unacceptable and even radical. In fact, for their dedicated efforts in launching the national campaign to establish the precursor to today's Maternal and Child Health programs, these women were maligned by their opposition as "subversives, communists, endocrine perverts and derailed menopausics" (Siefert, 1983).

In the implementation of this law, social work was introduced as the direct result of pressure from a committee headed by Edith Baker of the American Association of Medical Social Workers. The Children's Bureau acceded to the request of the committee for inclusion of Medical Social Work on the staff of the newly created Maternal and Child Health programs. Baker later was appointed the first chief of Medical Social Work in Maternal and Child Health and Crippled Children's Services. Since that time, it was federal policy to insist, first that all states employ medical social workers in the Crippled Children's program and later in the other Maternal and Child Health programs (Abbott, 1938). This network of maternal and child health social workers still exists today and is instrumental in developing guidance and standards for social work services in federally funded primary care programs.

In 1935, the passage of the Social Security Act, which included Maternal and Child Health and Crippled Children's Services, brought social work into primary care programs nationally. Previously, there were no social workers practicing in these settings except in Massachusetts and Los Angeles, which had social workers employed on the state and local level respectively.

Federal involvement in establishing formal primary care programs in the United States began with the Community Health Center program (Section 330 of the PHS Act, PL 95:62), which grew from two related activities in the 1960s:

1. The Office of Economic Opportunity Neighborhood Health Center Act (authorized by the 1966 Economic Opportunity Act, as part of President Lyndon B. Johnson's War on Poverty, and administered by OEO).
2. The Section 314(e) Health Center Act (authorized by the 1966 Amendments to the Public Health Service Act).

The Migrant Health Center program was first authorized within the United States Public Health Service (Section 340 of the PHS Act) in

1962. It specifically targeted migrant and seasonal agricultural workers who, because of their mobility, poverty, and minority cultures, lacked access to adequate health care. The program was reauthorized in 1975, and again in 1981 (*Primary Care Information Guide*).

During the mid-1970s, PHS began a Rural Health Initiative (RHI) and an Urban Health Initiative (UHI), (PL 95:62, section 330) as a focus of activity within the Community Health Center program. These special efforts combined limited grant resources in small health centers with health professionals assigned through the National Health Service Corps to attack the special problems of the medically underserved in health manpower shortage areas in rural and urban communities (*Primary Care Information Guide*).

The broad goals and objectives of both the Migrant and Community Health Center programs are to provide for children, adolescents, and adults — in urban and rural medically underserved areas — a comprehensive program of quality, family-oriented primary care health care services that:

- are easily accessible regardless of income, cultural background, geographic location, or physical disability
- offer continuity of care over time
- are well integrated with secondary and tertiary hospital and specialty care as needed
- are provided with a team of health professionals to facilitate comprehensive care
- are efficiently managed at community-based primary care centers with local governing boards that assure responsiveness to local needs (*Primary Care Information Guide*).

In addition to the community health centers, the federal government was simultaneously funding start-up grants for HMOs (Title 13 of the Public Health Service Act) and Family Medicine Residency Programs.

The previously cited examples of the Children's Bureau and its contribution to the passage of the Sheppard-Towner Act and the 1960s movement culminating in the War on Poverty and the Economic Opportunity Act reflect a common value system shared by the social work profession and the field of primary care. Because these programs and social workers stress comprehensive care, social justice, and advocacy for the disadvantaged, they should be able to join forces to develop a more complete health care delivery system.

CONTINUING EDUCATION

Continuing professional education has been available to health care social workers for some time. In 1935, state and local programs were encouraged to provide educational leave for professional education to support part-time study by staff, in addition to in-service training programs. It was not until the 1946 amendments, however, that increased level of support was available to state and local maternal and child health programs for special training programs.

By 1947, the first Federal-State Grant-in-Aid-supported training program was opened at the Harvard School of Public Health. This was an interdisciplinary training program for physicians, nurses, nutritionists, and social workers in Maternal and Child Health (MCH). Similar training projects quickly followed at the Johns Hopkins School of Public Health, the University of California School of Public Health, the University of Pittsburgh Graduate School of Public Health, and others.

In addition, a training project supported through the Children's Bureau with the Massachusetts Department of Health, the three schools of social work, and the Harvard School of Public Health began in 1949. The purpose of the project was to increase opportunities for accredited field work training and for adding public health content in the teaching programs of schools of social work and other such projects supported by MCH. This effort was intended to increase interest and knowledge of public health and primary care among social workers and assist in meeting the shortage of social work personnel in primary care agencies.

The Division of Maternal and Child Health, within the U.S. Public Health Service, has continued the commitment of the Children's Bureau since 1949 to increase the number of qualified social workers in primary care through its training grants to schools of social work throughout the United States. This Division presently supports regional and national conferences for social workers in primary care and other health settings, in conjunction with schools of public health and schools of social work throughout the nation.

RESEARCH

Social workers in primary health care have found it essential to study the psychosocial needs of the individual and family and to collaborate on projects undertaken by related professions and other community agencies. Several studies have been conducted by Baker and others which have improved social work practice as well as the health status of the patients being served. Examples of such studies are:

1. A study of the relationship between public health nurses and medical social workers to improve case management services.
2. A study of tuberculosis placements to understand the efficacy of physician's recommendations.
3. A study of venereal disease case finding to determine the sources of infection. The study assisted the County Health Department in strengthening its case finding program to control venereal disease in Los Angeles County (Baker, 1953).
4. A national study of the cause of infant mortality conducted by the Children's Bureau in 1913.

Social work research in primary care is sparse and needs to be enlarged. Research is essential to confirm the efficacy of social work interventions, to add to the theoretical and knowledge base of the profession, and to improve the living conditions and health status of the patient population that is being served. Issues that need to be investigated include case management, multidiscipline care, continuity of care, access to care, infant mortality, and teen pregnancy. The following study of social work services in primary care is one example of the type of research that is needed.

RECENT SURVEY OF SOCIAL SERVICES IN PRIMARY CARE - REGION V

In 1985, a Primary Care Social Work Initiative was organized in Region V of the U.S. Public Health Service. A region-wide task force was convened to assess and improve the quantity and quality of social services provided in federally funded primary care projects throughout the region. A survey document was designed and distributed to all eligible projects as a partnership endeavor of the task force (the State Primary Care Association Directors of each state) and the regional office. The sample consisted of the federally funded primary care projects located in Region V, including the following states: Illinois, Indiana, Michigan, Minnesota, Ohio, and Wisconsin.

Of 69 eligible projects, responses were received from 63, yielding a response rate of 91% for completion of the survey questionnaire. The questionnaire included 20 items related to 1) the perceived extent of patient social problems; 2) current social service staffing patterns;

3) referral patterns with community health and social programs; 4) social services for specific populations; and 5) perceived needs for social services. The questionnaire also provided a comment section for open-ended suggestions related to the social service issue. The survey provided the following information:

- The majority of clients served came for prenatal, family planning/ gynecological, and infant, child, and adolescent services. Seventy-five to eighty% of clients needing social service interventions were women of childbearing age, infants, children and adolescents.
- Poverty, access to medical care, and problems of early childbearing and child rearing (adolescent pregnancy and parenthood) were perceived as the most pressing social service problems facing these populations. Substance abuse and nutritional deficiencies were documented as widespread, as were problems with parent-child relationships and transportation to health care.
- Only 25% of the centers employed a social service director, and only 19% employed MSW staff on site; 50% of the projects used other professionals or paraprofessionals to deal with the social service needs of their clients, with nursing the most frequently used discipline.

Twenty-one percent of respondents reported that they receive reimbursement for social services. While there may be potential for third-party reimbursement for social services, this critical issue requires further study to determine the various rules and regulations of third-party payers, because each state differs considerably regarding legislative and administrative practices. Before this can occur, social workers need to document their usefulness to the primary care setting and its patients.

Many of the questionnaire responses and comments documented that populations currently served have greater unmet needs than in past years because of increased unemployment, larger number of the poor and near poor seeking unreimbursed care, and fewer private or voluntary community resources that will accept these needier populations for care. Many of the written comments expressed frustration with this dilemma of greater needs for service at a time of fiscal constraints. It is essential that community health center projects find innovative ways to meet the needs of their target populations without the assurance of additional federal resources.

Because 80% of persons in need of social services were women, infants, children, and adolescents (MCH program) units in states should consider developing collaborative arrangements and share resources with the community health center programs.

Of the projects studied, 25 were rural primary care projects (as designated by criteria of the U.S. Public Health Service), 23 were urban primary care projects, and the remainder were migrant health projects. In regard to the extent and type of social problems identified, both rural and urban patients had serious difficulty with financial needs. Rural administrators responded that problems related to aging were the most widespread, while urban administrators identified adolescent pregnancy and parenthood as their predominant high-risk population. The majority of rural projects also reported problems of teen pregnancy, parenting, substance abuse, parent-child conflict, and transportation, however.

Survey information also indicated that rural social service staff were engaged in case management and referrals as their primary social service activity, closely followed by direct clinical services, community outreach, and consultation and education. The majority of both rural and urban respondents indicated their greatest staffing need was for provision of direct clinical services. Urban administrators were nearly twice as likely as rural administrators were, however, to express needs for expanded social service administration, advocacy, and program evaluation activities.

Rural social service programs generally were understaffed and more likely to have staff with insufficient professional education (Young & Doss-Martin, in press).

What is apparent from the survey is that patients have significant needs for social work services but community health centers have not had the resources to hire staff to meet those needs. After the survey, many community health centers did receive additional funds to provide case management services to perinatal patients and to provide services to the homeless under the Stewart B. McKinney Act (PL 100:27). Many of these programs have used these additional funds to establish new social work developments or upgrade their existing departments.

CONCLUSION

A social work historian observed:

In studying the history of social work in health settings, I was struck with the same issue which I notice in contemporary practice. Social workers do not see crises as opportunities for gathering professional strength. In crisis situations when there is little treatment but social treatment, such as in the recent situations of Alzheimer's and AIDS, we are often prominent care takers. It seems we worry terribly about our clients but we do not negotiate from a position of strength. Instead, when the crisis abates because of a dramatic medical solution as in the cases of syphilis or polio, or when other professionals decide there is something they want to do here, we return power or have it taken from us.

Traditionally for the profession of social work, a public health crisis has not been a favorable juncture of circumstances, a good chance to increase professional strength. Rather, such crises have been seen as emergencies to which to respond altruistically, opportunities to confirm values. (Kerson, 1986)

A key lesson of the past is that social work has been greatly strengthened when advocates have insisted that our profession become a program requirement through legislative or regulatory mandate. For example, 20 million dollars was recently made available to community health centers to expand their perinatal programs to include case management services provided by social workers. The guidance to include social work in this initiative was provided in part by the network of social workers who once worked in the old Children's Bureau. Many social workers will be employed and many patients will benefit as a result of this effort.

Another lesson is that social workers must be involved in both direct services to patients and in leadership roles that affect legislation, regulations, standards, policy, and guidance. If we accomplish these two goals, social workers will continue to have an active role in the primary care programs in the future.

REFERENCES

Abbott, G. (1938). Organizing for administration of child welfare services. *The Child and the State, Vol. II.* Chicago.
Baker, E. M. (Ed.). (1953). *Medical social services for children in the Maternal and Child Health and Crippled Children's programs.* Washington, DC: U.S. Department of Health, Education and Welfare, Social Security Administration, Children's Bureau.
BCHS (1984). *Primary care information guide.* Rockville, MD: Bureau of Community Health, Delivery and Assistance.
Bradbury, D. E. (1962). *Five decades of action for children: A history of the children's bureau.* Washington, DC: U.S. Department of Health, Education and Welfare, Social Security Administration, Children's Bureau.

Encyclopedia of Social Work (16th ed.). (1971). New York: National Association of Social Workers (pp. 552-560).

Evans, J. C. (1983). Public health social work in maternal and child health. In A. Gitterman (Ed.), *The family in health care today* (p. 5). Conference proceedings of the Columbia University School of Social Work and Social Work Departments of Harlem, Morristown Memorial, Mt. Sinai, New York State Psychiatric Institute, Presbyterian-St. Lukes, Roosevelt Hospitals, New York.

Kerson, T. S. (1986, September). *Negotiating from strength: Mandates 'for practice in public health and hospital based social work.* Paper presented at the Annual Conference of the American Public Health Association, Las Vegas, NV.

O'Hara, D. (1978). An overview of training for social work in maternal and child health. In Y. H. Appel (Ed.), *The incorporation of MCH content into health concentrations in schools of social work* (pp. 7-15). Conference proceedings of the Graduate School of Social Work, Rutgers University, New Brunswick, NJ.

Siefert, K. (1983). An exemplar of primary prevention: The Sheppard-Towner Act of 1921. *Social Work in Health Care, 9*(1). 87-103.

Torrens, P.R. (1984). Historical evolution and overview of health services in the United States. In S. J. Williams & P. R. Torrens (Eds.), *Introduction to health services* (2nd ed.), (pp. 3-31). New York: John Wiley.

Young, C. L. & Doss-Martin, L. (in press). Social services in rural and urban primary care projects. *Human Services in the Rural Environment.* Chaney: University of East Washington.

FURTHER READING

Bracht, N. F. (Ed.). (1978). *Social work in health care: A guide to professional practice.* New York: Haworth.

Bullough, V. L., & Bullough, B. (1982). *Health care for the other Americans.* New York: Appleton-Century-Crofts.

Cabot, R. C. (1915). *Social service and the art of healing.* New York: Moffat, Yard.

Gorman, J. F., Varela, A. M. (Eds.). (1966). *Multidisciplinary practice in public health.* Conference proceedings of the 1965 Annual Institute for Public Health Social Workers. Berkeley: School of Public Health, School of Social Welfare, University of California.

Henk, M. (1982, November) *Improving prevention services through the integration of categorical programs into the primary care setting.* Paper presented at the Annual Conference of the American Public Health Association, Montreal, Canada.

Hull, J. B. (1986, June 3). Growing number in U.S. lack health insurance as companies, public agencies seek to cut costs. *The Wall Street Journal*, p. 54.

Insley, V. I. (1951, May). *Home care medical program to meet the needs of individuals and families.* Paper presented at the Annual Meeting of the National Conference of Social Work, Atlantic City, NJ.

Insley, V. I. (1977). Health services: maternal and child health. In J. B. Turner (Ed.), *Encyclopedia of social work.* Washington, DC: National Association of Social Workers.

Kumabe, K. T., Nishida, C., & Hepworth, D. H. (Eds.). (1985). *Bridging ethnocultural diversity in social work and health.* Honolulu School of Social Work, University of Hawaii.

Miller, R. S. (Ed). (1983). *Primary health care: More than medicine.* Englewood Cliffs, NJ: Prentice-Hall.

Morton, C. J. (1985). Public health social work priorities in maternal and child health. In A. Gitterman, R. B. Black, & F. Stein (Eds.), *Public health social work in maternal and child health: A forward plan* (pp. 41-64). New York: Columbia University School of Social Work.

Papers (1939). Given at the meetings of the American association of medical social workers, Menasha, WI: George Banta.

Parker, A. W. (1974). The dimensions of primary care: Blueprints for change. In S. Andreopoulos (Ed.), *Primary care: Where medicine fails* (pp. 15-76). New York: John Wiley.

Rauch, J. B. (Ed.). (1981). *Applied social work research in maternal and child health: Instrument for change.* Conference proceedings of the Philadelphia Regional Pediatric Pulmonary Disease Program, Philadelphia, PA.

Rice, R. G. (Ed.). (1956). *Commonwealth, 4*(6). Boston: Massachusetts Department of Public Health.

Rutigliano, A. J. (1985, October). Surgery on health care costs. *Management Review,* p. 32.

St. Denis, G. C. (Ed.). (1979). *Social work in primary health care.* Proceedings, 1979 Medical Social Consultants Meeting, U.S. Department of Health, Education, and Welfare, Bureau of Community Health Services, Maternal and Child Health Services, Pittsburgh, PA.

Schlesinger, E. G. (1985). *Health care social work practice: Concepts and strategies.* St. Louis, MI: Times Mirror/Mosby.

Soule, T. H. (1955). *The years 1916-1929. Selected papers and reports; fiftieth anniversary celebration.* Boston: Social Service Department, Massachusetts General Hospital.

White, G. (Ed.). (1944, September). Bulletin. *The American Association of Medical Social Workers, 17*(4).

Chapter 2

THE INTEGRATION OF PRIMARY HEALTH CARE AND SOCIAL WORK IN THE EDUCATIONAL SETTING

Lann E. Thompson
Howard J. Hess

INTRODUCTION

Since its inception, social work has been devoted to prevention and control of epidemics and debilitating diseases. The social work profession began near the end of the nineteenth century as part of social reform movements initiated by charitable organizations and settlement houses. Efforts were made to help the poor, the immigrant, the disenfranchised, the disabled, and the sick. By the turn of the century a new dimension of practice effort evolved along with a burgeoning public health movement. The profession focused on the person-in-the-situation, the dynamic interaction between the individual's physical and psychosocial well-being, or health and welfare. The role of social work in primary health care emerged as one part of an effort to overcome political, economic, social, and cultural barriers that endangered the health and welfare of populations at risk.

Social work in health care grew most rapidly in hospital settings. During its early history, medical social work understood that a patient's social situation is intrinsically tied to his/her physical well-being. Margolis (1949) writes:

The concept of homeostasis or physiological equilibrium in the individual cannot be limited to consideration of purely physical phenomena. For the human organism cannot be considered an isolated specimen in a hermetically sealed environment, but rather as an integral part of the wider milieu from which he stems and in which he lives. (p. 1)

Recently, a major role of social work in health care has been to place practitioners in ambulatory or primary care settings, including family practice, pediatrics, and internal medicine group practices. Consequently, the need to integrate social work training and primary health care has grown increasingly as an important educational issue over the last 15 years.

Nonetheless, social work in primary health care is a relatively new specialty. Kissel (1979) notes that social work is far from becoming a routine component of primary health care nationwide. Estimates by Hookey (1978), including only clinics or centers with three or more physicians, suggest that only three percent had social work participation. New initiatives are clearly needed to further integrate training in primary health care and social work.

This chapter reviews the history of social work training, which is relevant to practice in primary health care settings. Social work education in health care is reviewed with emphasis on the basic knowledge and skills necessary to integrate with primary health care in the educational setting. The authors present an interactional framework for assessment in social work and health care, followed by a shared training model. The shared training model seeks to bridge the current gaps in knowledge and skill for better integration of primary health care and social work in the educational setting. An overview of current trends in health care is presented with educational implications for social work. Finally, recommendations are made for implementing the shared training model.

HISTORICAL OVERVIEW: PRIMARY CARE AND SOCIAL WORK TRAINING

Stoeckle (1983) provides an excellent review tracing the origins of training in primary care and social work from the 1900s to the 1980s. Primary care is not a new idea. In 1905, Cabot proposed a novel treatment method focusing on group rather than solo practice and advocated that professional and interprofessional training include physicians, social workers and psychologists.

Education and training in primary care has occurred in large teaching hospitals with primary care residency programs, social work departments, and social work students involved in field placements. The interrelationships that developed within this type of practice setting have provided an opportunity for teamwork and interdisciplinary practice. Legislation in 1965 authorized Health and Human Services and the Division of Maternal and Child Health (DMCH) to fund specific projects to provide interdisciplinary training for practice related to services for children with multiple handicaps and mental retardation. A national network of over 20 University Affiliated Facilities (UAF) continues to provide this interdisciplinary health care training related to children and youth with special needs. Core curriculum for training social workers in UAF projects was published in 1976 (see McGrath, O'Hara, & Thomas). The curriculum contains little content on primary care.

Other DMCH projects that adopted the UAF interdisciplinary practice and training model are eight Pediatric Pulmonary Care Centers and six Adolescent Health Training Projects. Typically, these training projects are located within a medical school, the faculties represent various health care disciplines, and both exemplary service and interdisciplinary training are provided with students completing field practicums.

Apart from pediatric settings, many other model programs have provided training for health care professionals within family practice residency programs and in internal medicine residencies. The National Institute of Mental Health has awarded funding to train social workers in rural primary care settings. Woodward (1983) presents a comprehensive review of the major federal health care models. Davis (1983) observes that the majority of primary care delivery programs come from community health and migrant health programs.

Furthermore, Stoeckle (1983) cites a recent shift of emphasis on training physicians in primary care: "In internal medicine, 130 of 407 residencies (32%) have primary care tracts with 2,444 out of 16,531 residents, while family practice programs have 6,420 residents in training, and pediatrics, 5,301" (p. 141). No data were available on the number of social workers in these programs.

Turning specifically to training in schools of social work with health concentrations, Caroff and Mailick (1985) surveyed the 85 graduate schools of social work, with 72 responding. In the survey, 42 schools, or 58% of the respondents, reported basic health concentrations with only 11 schools having health concentrations by 1975. No specific information was obtained on the primary care content within the various health concentrations. Black (1985) completed an additional survey that focused directly on curricular coverage of public health and maternal and child health content. She surveyed 52 graduate schools of social work listed by the Council of Social Work Education for having students specializing in health care practice. A total of 41 schools (78.8%) responded, with 32 of those schools offering a health-related specialization. In surveying the schools on five basic public health concepts (epidemiological rates; populations-at-risk; relative and attributable risks; multicausality of disorders, that is, agent, host, and environment; and preventive interventions) she found that only a few schools were providing "little or no content." Black concluded that most students in health concentrations were still receiving traditional, clinical training in social work practice with minor emphasis on skills important to social work in public health.

Black's survey also assessed curricular content specific to maternal and child health in 13 subject areas—pregnancy; human sexuality; family planning; parenting; genetic counseling; effects of death and bereavement on young children, parents, and siblings; developmental disabilities; premature infants; chronically ill/physically disabled children; neglected and abused children; children with serious behavioral or emotional disorders; adolescents at risk for problems such as pregnancy, substance abuse or suicide; and legal issues in family planning. The responses suggested substantial variation in content coverage with a majority reporting at least some content in all of the 13 subject areas. Unfortunately, few of the subject areas received extensive coverage across all the schools. A number of schools reported little or no attention given to some of these topics.

In summary, the literature review revealed minimal integration of primary health care and social work in the educational setting, and a lack of clearly specified curricula in the classroom and the field. Before a proposed model to foster better integration is presented, the core knowledge base and skills for specialization in social work and health care will be reviewed from the current literature with emphasis on primary care.

SOCIAL WORK EDUCATION FOR HEALTH CARE: CORE KNOWLEDGE AND BASIC SKILLS

Review of the social work education literature revealed an emphasis on preparing social workers for generic health care roles on an interdisciplinary team (Kane, 1975). The social worker's role on the interdisciplinary team is to identify patient/system needs from the concrete resource/advocacy level to the abstract psychosocial/counseling level. The social worker on the team must act as a change agent: as a source of information/referral and/or direct service to provide growth-producing interventions that improve social functioning. Social workers must use a variety of methods. Typical roles range from the generic/generalist to the technical/clinical specialist and include broker, technical expert, educator, diagnostician, counselor/therapist, coordinator, supervisor, consultant, administrator, planner, developer, advocate, and researcher (Doremus, 1976).

The combination and range of roles of the social worker on the health care team is shaped by the agency's setting, goals, and function in the community. Kumabe, Nishida, O'Hara, and Woodruff (1977) characterize the social worker's primary role in the community health care setting as systemic in nature: that is, a role that enables consumers to use the health care system successfully. Social workers should intervene with both patients and the interdisciplinary team to enhance their complementary roles. They also can provide valuable information on designing and changing health care systems. Chaiklin (1976) states that social workers should address all the psychosocial problems which patients bring to the health care setting, focusing on relationships among physical, social, emotional, and cultural factors that influence patient/system behavior. He also placed major emphasis on social workers' expertise in community resources and service coordination. Although the literature has outlined multiple areas of responsibility for social workers in health care settings (Germain, 1984), the core knowledge and skills needed to do the job are not clearly defined.

CORE KNOWLEDGE

Core knowledge for social work practice in health settings requires competency in five areas: human behavior and the social environment, social welfare policy and services, social work practice, research, and the field practicum (Council on Social Work Education, 1982). Content in these areas provides for the integration of theory and practice for social work in health care. The social worker needs to understand the nature of disease and subsequent medical treatment. In addition to this core knowledge, the worker providing comprehensive care in the community health setting needs a specialty knowledge in public health social work. Gorman (1977, p. 36) identifies areas of specialty knowledge for public health social work as:

1. Individual and community health behavior.
2. Health service systems in the United States (the history, trends, problems, funding).
3. Public health concepts and approaches including basics of sociodemographics and epidemiology (the epidemiological intervention model, or the host-agent relationship).
4. Social work practice in health settings (prevention, interprofessional practice, administration, consultation).
5. Social, cultural, and emotional aspects of health and illness.

Distinct skills at the micro- and macrosystem levels are necessary for social workers to function competently in primary care programs. Social work field training in an interdisciplinary setting is critical to the integration of knowledge, values, and methods/skills in developing a comprehensive, competency-based practice in primary health care. What, then, should be the minimum level of skill on completion of field training?

BASIC SKILLS

The community-based social worker in a comprehensive health care setting must have diverse practice skills drawn from a knowledge of public health and social work disciplines. Solid diagnostic and assessment skills are prerequisite to effective social work interventions (Coulton, 1981). To intervene at the microsystem level of primary care, the social worker should be able to:

1. Identify risk factors and develop interventions to reduce the risk.
2. Provide information, referral and education for the patient.
3. Provide ongoing clinical diagnosis, assessment, and counseling for psychosocial problems encountered by the patient and family across the life cycle.
4. Tailor an individual service plan to the patient and family.
5. Coordinate and implement interdisciplinary services that ensure continuity-of-care and avoid fragmentation and duplication of services.
6. Follow up and monitor individual service plans.
7. Document and evaluate the provision of services.
8. Maintain standards of care through quality assurance and case review activity.

To intervene at the macrosystem level of primary care, the social worker should have basic skills in the following areas:

1. Casefinding, screening, diagnostic, assessment, and evaluation models for patients and their families.
2. Collaborative practice skills at the group, organizational, and community levels.
3. Advocacy, negotiation, and facilitation skills in dealing with legislative and regulatory systems that affect patients and their families.
4. Skill in community education and organization that involves planning for services at the local, state, regional, or national levels.
5. Consultation with other professionals, parents, and volunteers working with patients and their families.
6. Supervisory and managerial skills in service delivery, monitoring, accountability, evaluation, grant writing, quality assurance, and research.

Quality intervention skills in social work at any level of health care demand an assessment of need for service. The assessment should follow a professionally recognized model or theoretical framework that can identify need and risk factors both qualitatively and quantitatively. A theoretical framework for assessment is necessary to synthesize and to integrate the social worker's generic and specialty knowledge into effective assessment and intervention. Without a solid theoretical model or framework, the likely result is a loose collection of practice wisdom that cannot be empirically tested and validated to further extend and refine the public health social work knowledge base.

INTERACTIONAL FRAMEWORK FOR ASSESSMENT

The traditional theoretical framework for social work assessment has been psychodynamically oriented, but recently has shifted to ecological systems theory (Germain & Gitterman, 1980). Because ecological systems theory is more comprehensive, it affords more flexibility for integration of knowledge from multiple sources with benefit of differential interventions (Germain, 1984). Systems theory allows incorporation of ecological and epidemiological principles as applied to public health social work methods of assessment and intervention. Systems theory is dynamic and interlocks well with stress-adaptation theory and developmental theory. Together, these three theories are valuable for social work assessment and intervention. Indeed, this new interactional framework has tremendous capacity for synthesizing, describing and quantifying the problems of primary health care patients and their families.

To apply the proposed interactional framework at a microsystems level, the social worker must interview the patient and the family for qualitative information about the patient/family stress-adaptation patterns, patient/family developmental status, and patient/family system and environment (the organizational structure, roles, reactions, resources, relationship, level of functioning and their community). Quantitative assessment to determine risk factors and service needs can be done with stress/coping inventories (McCubbin & Patterson, 1981), developmental scales (Cross & Goin, 1977), and family system and environmental inventories (Olson, McCubbin, Barnes, Larsen, Muxen, & Wilson, 1982). Because fiscal and time constraints do not always permit a complete assessment, these scales and inventories can be invaluable screening tools in quantifying risk factors and defining psychosocial acuity.

Psychosocial acuity refers to the patient/family psychosocial condition, and the subsequent degree of need for social work services (Coulton, Keller, & Boone, 1985). Drawing from observations, patient and family interviews, developmental scales, stress adaptation, and system inventories, the worker can quickly profile the data and information. Qualitatively and quantitatively the profile identifies psychosocial problems, risk factors, resources and strengths per child/family stress-adaptation patterns, patient/family developmental status, and family system and environmental factors.

Within the interactional framework (systems theory, stress-adaptation theory, developmental theory) a multidimensional assessment can be organized with a comprehensive social work action plan by developmental needs, stress-adaptation needs and family system/environmental needs according to the problems, vulnerabilities, resources, and strengths for each area of need. In the formulation of an individualized service plan, the social worker needs to present an assessment to the health care team that ensures interventions are clearly matched to developmental, stress-adaptation, and family system needs. Thus, the social worker has a comprehensive blueprint to devise and implement preventive and rehabilitative treatment strategies.

In contrast, social work assessment at a macrosystems level must involve sociodemographic and epidemiological analysis of health care problems for specific at-risk population groups rather than assessing singular patient/family cases. Incidence and prevalence rates are determined; service delivery programs are planned; policies are established that meet the total individual needs for large patient groups in the context of their families and communities. The resultant programs and policies need evaluation for efficiency and effectiveness coupled with accountability procedures and standards of care. Community education and advocacy are also necessary to attain funding and appropriate legislation for program and policy implementation.

In assessing need for service at the macrosystems level, the social worker likewise can apply the interactional theoretical framework (stress-adaptation theory, system theory and developmental theory) as described above. Applying the interactional theoretical framework on a collective basis, the social worker can qualitatively and quantitatively analyze the common stress-adaptation patterns for at-risk groups of patients and their families. From a developmental perspective, the social worker also can collect and review data for common vulnerabilities or periodic stressors across the life cycle for the high-risk patient groups. The worker can thereby establish high-risk points in the continuum-of-care that will demand more intensive service for prevention of and intervention at developmental crisis points. On a systems basis, the worker must assess apparent trends in family systems and community systems that are either a benefit or a detriment to patients and their families. From the assessment data, high-risk family and community profiles can be targeted for program planning and policy analysis, such as for the AIDS population.

Understandably, social workers in primary health care must better articulate measurable outcomes for populations at risk. Impact assessment should evaluate the extent to which the program creates desired changes in the target population. Program cost-benefit and cost-effectiveness measures are also necessary to program planning. Before implementation, program monitoring and accountability measures should stipulate the assessment measures that will monitor program interventions for consonance with the program design within adequate standards of care. In any program, a representative sample of individual case audits is necessary for quality assurance procedure to lead to formation of corrective action plans that improve social work assessment and intervention in the delivery of primary health care.

Unfortunately, most professional training for practice in primary health care is still organized by discipline, without sufficient regard for interdisciplinary interaction. For example, the training of primary care physicians emphasizes medical treatment with limited attention to behavioral aspects of medical treatment. Unique to social work training is the emphasis on psychosocial intervention within a public health framework. Traditionally, these two training approaches to health care are taught independently rather than jointly. A joint approach would enhance the integration of primary health care and social work in field training with physicians and other health care professionals. A shared training model is needed to integrate the medical and behavioral science knowledge base with the psychosocial and public health social work knowledge base.

The proposed shared training model rests on a continuum of practice activities shared by physicians, health care givers, and social workers while other interventions remain discipline-specific. The model is best implemented by interdisciplinary field training experience that promotes prevention and wellness for both specific patients (microsystems) and specific populations (macrosystems). The model expands the current strengths within medical and social work training. The resultant integration of psychosocial concepts from both the behavioral science and public health perspectives offers diverse social work interventions in primary health care.

PROPOSED SHARED TRAINING MODEL

The professional training of social workers and that of physicians in primary health care differ considerably from one another. Physicians learn to treat diseases, and their medical training emphasizes distinct application of the scientific method to primarily biological problems. Physicians generally are trained to reduce problems to a diagnostic condition that is treated in highly specific ways. Consistent with Western medical practice, physicians receive a biological base for practice in which a variety of methods are used to measure patient functioning.

Recently, primary care physicians have also received exposure to the behavioral sciences in their training. Although the nature and extent of this exposure varies widely, the behavioral science base tends to expand on the physician's understanding of and flexibility with an individual patient. Many primary care physicians, for example, have been taught microinterviewing skills for use in the medical interview. In addition, medical training in primary care specialties such as family medicine has included psychiatric rotations and other experiences

Table 2.1

Patient	
Primary Care Physician (Medical & Behavioral Science Base)	Primary Care Social Worker (Psychosocial/Public Health Base)

designed to improve comprehension of patients' psychological functioning. However, this psychological focus has tended to be narrowly defined in terms of compliance with medical treatment. In some specialized training projects, greater attention has been given to developing a more comprehensive behavioral science base. Areas in which primary care physicians might receive special training have included stress management, biofeedback, hypnosis, sexual counseling, and behavior modification. It is also possible that primary care physicians have had exposure to family treatment, including both marital and parent-child counseling.

Although primary care physicians have had exposure to behavioral sciences, they view patient needs very differently from the way in which social workers view them. As suggested in Table 2.1, the practice base for each profession is distinct.

Typically, the nature of the primary health care setting supports and flows from the physician's perception of patient care. One aspect of physicians' training stresses their need for control in the health setting. The "right of referral" prerogative often reflects physicians' strong senses of ownership with regard to patient care. Although it is commonly understood that no single profession can adequately respond to all patient needs, physicians and social workers continue to have difficulty devising a model of shared patient care that emphasizes patient need rather than professional training. We propose a shared model of primary care training that builds on existing professional strengths and integrates biological, behavioral, and social science content.

Built on core knowledge and skills in social work and health care, this model emphasizes both shared patient care and shared professional training in primary health care. Patient care activities remain the central organizing feature of the model in which tasks are located along the continuum in Table 2.2.

As suggested by the continuum, multiple concurrent tasks and sequential tasks tend to characterize primary patient care. This model recognizes the complexity of patient care and proposes to systematize professional areas of responsibility between professions. Conse-

Table 2.2

Physician		*Social Worker*
Medical Decision-Making	Shared Tasks	Community Linkage

Table 2.3

Physician				*Social Worker*
Medical Treatment	Monitoring of Short-Term Treatment and Patient Compliance	Interviewing Patient Stress Management	Intervention with Families	Practice with At-Risk Patients and Culturally Diverse Patients; Information, Referral, and Advocacy with Community Resources

quently, professional training must provide the skill base for effective interdisciplinary practice.

NATURE OF PROFESSIONAL CONTINUUM

The continuum of patient care tasks reserves certain tasks for physicians and others for social workers. Patient care issues related to medical decision-making, for example, clearly remain the physician's responsibility while tasks related to patient care in the community remain with the primary care social worker. Each discipline must understand the nature of those tasks and participate supportively because the tasks are not interchangeable. Many other patient care tasks in the primary care setting, however, require collaboration and shared decision-making. The degree of leadership in task completion supplied by the physician or social worker is determined by how closely the tasks fall within each professional domain. For example, as Table 2.3 suggests, in-office monitoring of patient compliance, particularly on a short-term basis, is closely related to the physician's plan of patient care whereas the inclusion of patients' families in the primary care plan demands that the social worker focus attention beyond the individual patient. The greater the intersection between the patient's medical and

Table 2.4

Physician		Social Worker
Establish Short-Term Goals and Plans	Intervene in Dysfunctional Lifestyle Patterns and Health Care	Monitor When Necessary and Intervene in Health Care Usage Patterns

psychosocial needs, the more likely the physician and social worker will collaborate on a given case.

The continuum also considers continuity of care over time. Given the nature of primary health care in the United States, the likelihood of most patients being treated by the same physician over an extended period of time is decreasing. Particularly in settings such as family medicine centers, outpatient clinics, and group practices, social workers and other health professionals are more likely to develop long-term familiarity with a given patient than are physicians. Consequently, social workers are often in a better position to comprehend and to monitor long-term patterns of patient lifestyle and compliance. As Table 2.4 suggests, social workers can be expected to contribute to primary and secondary disease prevention.

The shared training model proposes that clarity of responsibility for patient care is the basis for designing an effective field curriculum for training in primary care. Patient care that involves medical case management and short-term response to patient distress is usually the physician's responsibility. Tasks related to communities, family mobilization, continuity of care, and prevention of health problems are viewed as the social worker's responsibility. Quality patient care is a blend of the two and is shared among physicians and social workers who may alternate leadership and decision-making responsibilities.

NATURE OF PROFESSIONAL TASKS

This model stresses the functions of education and patient motivation. Motivation frames the patient's ability to contribute to the care plan, while education is a professional activity with the individual patients, families, and other health care professionals. The goal of the model is to enhance patient care through the development of fun-

Table 2.5

Physician		Shared			Social Worker
Decision about Medical Diagnosis, Testing, Medication	Patient Education	Patient Counseling	Family Treatment	Compliance Review over an Extended Time	Prevention of Gaps in Continuity of Care

damental professional skills. For the physician, skills of medical diagnosis are essential in devising patient care plans that account for patient need and available technology. Further, the model emphasizes the physician's selective use of self in influencing successful adoption of the patient role. Table 2.5 suggests that the physician's effect is greater at the time of initial medical diagnosis and subsequent medical crisis. The quality of subsequent care depends on the physician's accurate problem definition at the onset of care. Information supplied by the social worker regarding the patient's psychosocial situation can assist but cannot replace the primary care physician's responsibility to assess a patient's medical needs.

Once an accurate diagnosis and patient care plan are established, the steps for implementing the plan involve multiple-care decisions. Because efficient and effective primary health care requires maximum patient and family participation, community supports, and continuity of care across health care systems, the model stresses the importance of these three areas.

To educate patients, physicians and social workers must share accurate information in a timely manner. The literature recognizes a gap between the information health care professionals have about patients and the information patients have and understand about themselves. This model expects physicians to share information with patients, relate the information to realistic health care plans, and present these plans to patients and their families. Furthermore, physicians are expected to educate other health care professionals, including social workers, so that helpful monitoring and follow-up can take place. When many patients or family education is involved, or when patient education alone is insufficient, the care plan becomes the social worker's responsibility. The social worker's task then becomes one of either counseling the patient/family, providing patient education, or referring the patient to a counseling resource. The social worker's responsibility to monitor and assess the ongoing needs for patient education is often essential to successful primary care.

Regarding patient motivation, this model recognizes the crucial importance of patients' ability to support their own wellness. However, this aspect of patient behavior is only partially understood. The shared authority in the model encourages patients and their families to be full participants in the health care process and expects them to seek and use available supports to protect their own well-being. The physician promotes patient responsibility by providing high-quality medical care, conveying patient respect, and sharing appropriate information. The social worker should intervene when compliance is insufficient or doubtful. A differential assessment by the social worker regarding noncompliance should provide direction regarding follow-up needs. Referral and advocacy to obtain community resources are needed to ensure compliance with the health care plan. Where lack of compliance results from insufficient resources, referral and advocacy are helpful. When understanding is blocked by reactions such as anxiety or denial, counseling or similar interventions should be provided. In the process, social workers can assist physicians and other health professionals to detect and understand noncompliant behaviors.

Regarding prevention, the model strongly supports the notion that the primary health care system provides an excellent range of possibilities to detect and intervene with high-risk and vulnerable populations. It has been clearly documented that primary health care settings can provide necessary patient care before health problems require drastic interventions. Whether one is considering chronic disease, parent/child problems, or stress-related disease, a large proportion of later severe health problems are predictable in early patient encounters. The potential savings in health care costs from early detection provide primary health care with a worthy challenge. The social worker's role in assessing multiple psychosocial sources of disease within the community and bringing patients into the primary care system is another way to achieve prevention. With respect to primary prevention and continuity of care, the social worker should have knowledge and skills related to social resource networks.

SKILL BASE OF CONTINUUM MODEL

The proposed model requires differential skill usage for physicians, social workers, and other health care professionals. As presented in Table 2.6, the professional skills are an expression of the identified professional tasks. Integration of these skills allows educators to build curricula that reflect practice needs while identifying opportunities for collaborative training. For example, physicians must possess skills in medical diagnosis to access and interpret a range of diagnostic tests. They must also know about and be able to obtain needed pharmacology information. Also, physicians need training in three sets of interpersonal skills: those cognitive teaching skills related to information sharing; motivational skills related to influencing patient behavior; and leadership skills related to the functioning of the interdisciplinary health care team. These skills require both theoretical and experiential learning opportunities. For physicians, the learning will need to begin in medical school and continue in residency training.

For the social worker, interactional assessment skills are essential to an accurate social diagnosis. The social diagnosis needs to focus on psychosocial acuity, or risk, in order to determine the level of patient care needed within the primary health care program. After determination of acuity, social workers can more accurately predict both short- and long-term health futures for patients and devise a care plan accordingly. The requisite skill of psychosocial triage is also important. Social workers will need training to advocate for high-risk patients when health resources are limited. Immediacy of need and personal resources will affect the delivery of services. Advocacy skills are essential to the social work primary health care curriculum. Advocacy includes interventions on behalf of patients with all social systems including patient families, the primary health care organization, and other community resources. It also includes resource brokerage/mediation and skills related to motivating patients to act on their own behalf.

Social workers should assist patients in resolving psychosocial problems. The range of problems is vast and diverse. Sometimes social workers are required to provide crisis intervention or supportive counseling in the face of sudden trauma or catastrophic illness. During any intervention, social workers may need to help patients realistically confront their current illness or dysfunctional life-style patterns and structure a program of habit change. In these instances, social workers may provide inpatient education, stress reduction groups, or biofeed-

Table 2.6

(Small Group Problem-Solving Skills)			(Outreach and Motivational Skills)	
Medical Diagnosis	Cognitive Teaching Skills	Skills in Supportive and Psychosocial Counselling	Skills Advocacy in Family Treatment	Social Diagnosis

back. Numerous techniques and preplanned programs are available to the social worker. The purpose, however, is always to enhance patient wellness.

In some cases the social worker intervenes to ensure patient compliance and in other cases to ensure continuity of care. The social worker should have a better understanding than other health professionals would of a patient's history and psychosocial needs, and of available support systems. This knowledge enables social workers to intervene intermittently over time at critical points in a patient's life. The skill of the social worker lies in 1) selecting those crucial intervention points; 2) intervening effectively and efficiently; and 3) mobilizing resources in the patient's life span, including family and social networks. In this way the social worker addresses a range of important psychosocial needs that often extend beyond the immediate medical diagnosis.

An area of training related to interdisciplinary practice is needed and should be shared by both medicine and social work. Activities necessary to foster team building and case collaboration require many specific skills. Beginning with information-sharing skills as noted earlier, both professional groups need to know how to teach each other that portion of their own professional skills that is useful to the other. Social workers, for example, can enhance both effectiveness and efficiency in primary care by teaching physicians general advocacy skills. Conversely, the social worker's skill at monitoring patient compliance and engaging in patient education is strengthened when the physician teaches selective medical knowledge.

An exchange of skills is most likely to occur within an interdisciplinary team or work group. Such work groups do not necessarily evolve naturally but require organizational skills related to program design, role delineation, and conflict management. Given the difference in earlier training and professional perspectives, interdisciplinary practice skills require team building and shared leadership built upon a supportive organizational base. This is important especially in primary health care settings in which the flow of patients and the demand for quick, accurate decisions produce high levels of stress. The proposed shared training model suggests a professional training curriculum for both medicine and social work. The curriculum is based on the premise that primary health care is one aspect of a much larger health care system. Discipline-specific curricula and interdisciplinary curricula presume also that primary health care can play a major role in health promotion and disease prevention. Based on these overall principles, it is crucial that part of the professional training for primary care physicians and social workers provide an integration of practicum experiences. As such, interdisciplinary teaming and case collaboration can occur before the onset of full professional demands.

Social work training has gaps in the areas of biological knowledge, pharmacology, and to a certain extent, decision-making in health care organization. These shortcomings may make it difficult for social workers to relate sufficiently their psychosocial interventions to a primary health focus. Consequently, social workers may not be able fully to evaluate the effect of disease process, evaluative testing, and medications. In fact, social workers historically have tended to detach themselves from the patient's medical treatment, claiming that medical care is not within their area of expertise. Such a view is short-sighted and limits the social worker's participation in preventive patient education and patient monitoring.

Shared gaps in professional training have resulted from the relative absence of training opportunities for interdisciplinary practice. Where students from multiple professions have trained together, shared decision-making processes have developed their skills in case sharing. Beyond the skills of case sharing there are many public health and service delivery issues to recognize in the provision of shared training.

CURRENT ISSUES AND HEALTH CARE TRENDS

Current issues affecting primary health care and social work training stem from policy and planning in public health care and current economic trends in the delivery of health care. In the fall of 1980 the U.S. Department of Health and Human Services, Public Health Service published *Promoting Health/Preventing Disease: Objectives for the Nation.* It presented a national strategy to achieve further improvement in the health of Americans by 1990. The impetus provided specific priorities under preventive health services, health protection, and health promotion. The national health strategy contains the following objectives:

Preventive health services
1. High blood-pressure control
2. Family planning
3. Pregnancy and infant health
4. Immunization
5. Sexually transmitted diseases

Health protection
1. Toxic agent control
2. Occupational safety and health
3. Accident prevention and injury control
4. Fluoridation and dental health
5. Surveillance and control of infectious diseases

Health promotion
1. Smoking and health
2. Misuse of alcohol and drugs
3. Nutrition
4. Physical fitness and exercise
5. Control of stress and violent behavior

Clearly, in the 1980s we are witnessing a radical restructuring of health delivery. This includes the elimination of entitlement programs, the reduction of federal policy regulations, greater spending control to states (block grants), stronger measures for health care cost containment (diagnostically related groups, or DRGs), and a greater emphasis on health care for profit (health maintenance organizations, preferred provider options, home health care agencies, ambulatory convenience care centers). (For example, see *Quality Of Care Under Medicare's Prospective Pricing System*, 1986; Reemer, 1985; and Rehr, 1984.)

As a result of this restructuring, primary health care delivery programs are more fragmented and have less money, yet they are asked to serve more patients with increased quality of care. The resulting economic trends that affect the delivery of primary care are summarized as follows:

1. Reduction of health care financial resources and strong emphasis on accountability and free marketing.

2. Greater expectations for increased productivity in health care delivery.
3. Reduced access to hospital resources and an increase in for-profit community health care.
4. Fewer resources for care of certain patient populations, such as the elderly, the chronically ill, the poor, and AIDS victims.
5. An increase in medical technology available to those who can afford it.
6. The need to address psychosocial issues in health care delivery (patient understanding, improving motivation, and compliance).

EDUCATIONAL IMPLICATIONS FOR SOCIAL WORK AND PRIMARY CARE

In response to spiraling health care costs that exceed inflation rates by 5 to 6 percent annually, a major revolution is under way to restructure health care delivery to contain costs. While health care costs continue to soar, funding for public health care programs will remain stationary at best or will decrease at worst. Inevitably, we are "hoping to do more with fewer dollars" and primary care offers a challenging opportunity to do so.

Advances in medical technology will cost more and will continue to create major ethical dilemmas in health care. Some examples are: If we can treat, should we treat? What are the patients' rights? What are the families' rights? How do we assure informed decision-making? Who will get the utmost in health care? What are acceptable standards of primary care for patients and their families? Who should benefit from new medical treatments and for how long? These are just some of the many difficult dilemmas we face.

The implications for integration of primary health care with social work education are obvious, immense, overwhelming, and challenging. Social workers will need to exert more and stronger advocacy to maintain necessary programs and services to at-risk populations. Prevention efforts at all levels of care need major emphasis to achieve greater benefit or the same benefit from limited program dollars. Screening and assessment tools should quantify psychosocial risk factors and target social work intervention on a proactive rather than a reactive basis. Social work standards in primary health care for patients and their families need clearer articulation and documentation. Networking, resource sharing, and collaboration among health and human service programs will become even more essential. Treatment protocols should be developed for prevention and early intervention for specific diseases. Protocols for social work in primary health care should focus psychosocial assessment and intervention on measurable target outcomes.

RECOMMENDATIONS

To advance development of the shared training model, curricula must educate not only social workers but physicians and other health care professionals about the mission, values, and aims of social work intervention in primary health care. Development of paid fellowships for interdisciplinary training in primary care settings would offer more opportunities to practice the shared training model. Field faculty need to become more involved in field education. Increasing joint faculty appointments across the health care disciplines would greatly enhance shared training, increase research opportunities, complement curricula, and aid development of subspecialty practice by specific population groups. Social work should take the lead in facilitating shared training. Specifically, social work curriculum in primary care should:

1. View clinical practice within the context of an interdisciplinary process with a major emphasis on health promotion and disease prevention.
2. Teach interventions for those at risk not only at a microsystem level (individuals and families) but also at a macrosystem level (specific populations).
3. Teach health care professionals and students the behavioral, ethnic, cultural, human development, biological, health care delivery, and environmental factors that affect health and health care delivery.
4. Be comprehensive and integrate the concepts of direct service, program planning/policy development, community organizations, social planning, consultation, and public health in shared training practicums.
5. Provide students with the skill to assess genetic, psychosocial, demographic, epidemiological, biomedical disease, behavioral, cultural, human development/life cycle, quality of life/self-determination, public health system, and economic and political factors for prevention at the microsystem and macrosystem levels.
6. Teach a wide range of shared interventions from the generic to the specific. This will require social work curriculum to develop practice subspecialties in primary health care, perhaps by specific population groups.
7. Study the costs and benefits of social work in primary care settings.
8. Be responsive to the current gaps and issues in health care delivery as identified in public health policy and planning literature.

9. Be sensitive to health care trends in the private sector.

10. Teach interdisciplinary interventions that share the common training objectives of improving the health status of all patients, lowering the incidence of chronic illness, and promoting conditions that reinforce wellness.

Notably, curriculum and field practice must develop quantitative and qualitative social work assessment skills. Preferably, routine usage of psychosocial acuity indices will evolve to establish the need for social work intervention and to provide productivity indicators to management for enhanced accountability and evaluation of social work service. Determination of psychosocial acuity can help to categorize social work primary care efforts and identify where staff and resources are best used. Even though social workers strive to help all patients, realistically they cannot; they must intervene effectively and efficiently to provide shared primary care.

In the final analysis, social work should take the leadership for shared training and for providing quality primary health care for high-risk populations. In the context of today's community-based health care, we must competitively market and deliver comprehensive social work services with clear standards for primary health care that will better serve patients and their families. We need the courage to create new ideas, to take calculated risks, and to advocate proactively for wellness rather than remain encumbered by the costly models of disease-oriented health care.

REFERENCES

Black, R. B. (1985). The state of the art in public health social work education: Public health and maternal child health content in graduate and continuing education programs. In A. Gitterman, R. B. Black, & F. Stein (Eds.), *Public health social work in maternal and child health: A forward plan.* New York: Columbia University School of Social Work.

Caroff, P., & Mailick, M. D. (1985). Health concentrations in schools of social work: The state of the art. *Health and Social Work, 10,* 5-14.

Chaiklin, H. (1976, June). *Needed: A generic definition of social work practice.* Paper presented at the National Conference on Social Welfare, Washington, DC.

Coulton, C. (1981). Person-environment fit as focus in health care. *Social Work,* Vol. 26(1).

Coulton, C., Keller, S. M., & Boone, C. R. (1985, January). Predicting social workers' expenditure of time with hospital patients. *Health and Social Work Journal, 10*(1), 35-44.

Cross, L., & Goin, K. (Eds.). (1977). *Identifying handicapped children: A guide to casefinding, screening, diagnosis, assessment and evaluation.* New York: Walker.

Curriculum Policy for the Master's Degree and Baccalaureate Degree Programs in Social Work Education (1982). Council on Social Work Education.

Davis, K. (1983). National policy in primary health care: Past, present, and future. In R. Miller (Ed.), *Primary health care, more than medicine.* Englewood Cliffs, NJ: Prentice-Hall.

Doremus, B. (1976). The four Rs: Social diagnosis in health care. *Health and Social Work, Vol. I(4),* 120-139.

Germain, C. B. (1984). *Social work practice in health care: An ecological perspective.* New York: Free Press.

Germain, C. B., & Gitterman, A. (1980). *The life model of social work practice.* New York: Columbia University Press.

Gorman, J. F. (1977). The incorporation of maternal and child health content into health concentrations in schools of social work. In Y. Appel (Ed.), *Designing and subspecialty in maternal and child health: Issues and core content.* New Brunswick, NJ: Rutgers Graduate School of Social Work.

Hookey, P. (1978). Social work in primary health care. In N. F. Bracht (Ed.), *Social work in health care: A guide to professional practice.* New York: Haworth.

Kane, R. (1975). *Interprofessional teamwork.* Syracuse, NY: Syracuse University, School of Social Work.

Kumabe, K., Nishida, C., O'Hara, D., & Woodruff, C. (1977). *A handbook for social work education and practice in community health settings.* Honolulu: School of Social Work, University of Hawaii.

Margolis, H. (1949). The biodynamic point of view in medicine. In *Casework approach to health problems,* pp. 1-7. New York: Family Service Association of America.

McCubbin, H., & Patterson, J. M. (1981). *Systematic assessment of family stress, resources, and coping, tools for research, education and clinical intervention.* St. Paul, MN: Family Social Science.

McGrath, F. C., O'Hara, D., & Thomas, D. (1976). *Graduate social work education in the university affiliated facility — Instructional manual and evaluation guide.* Miami, FL: University of Miami Mailman Center for Child Development.

Olson, D. H., McCubbin, H., Barnes, H., Larsen, A., Muxen, M., & Wilson, M. (1982). *Family inventories: Inventories used in a national survey of families across the family life cycle.* St. Paul: University of Minnesota Family Social Science.

Stoeckle, J. D. (1983). Curriculum development and training for health professionals: The job ahead. In R. S. Miller (Ed.), *Primary health care: More than medicine.* Englewood Cliffs, NJ: Prentice-Hall.

Woodward, K. (1983). The primary health care model. In R. S. Miller (Ed.), *Primary health care: More than medicine.* Englewood Cliffs, NJ: Prentice-Hall.

FURTHER READING

Bartlett, H. (1957). *Fifty years of social work in the medical setting.* New York: National Association of Social Workers.

Carlton, T. O. (1984). *Clinical social work in health setting.* New York: Springer.

Curriculum policy for the master's degree and baccalaureate degree programs in social work education. New York: CSWE.

Kane, R. S., & Rehr, H. (1975). *Social work issues in health care.* Englewood Cliffs, NJ: Prentice-Hall.

Miller, R. S. (Ed.). (1983). *Primary health care: More than medicine.* Englewood Cliffs, NJ: Prentice-Hall.

Promoting health/preventing disease: Objectives for the nation. (1980). U.S. Department of Health and Human Services, Public Health Services. Washington, DC: U.S. Government Printing Office.

Quality of care under Medicare's prospective payment system Vols. 1 and 2, Report of hearings before the Special Committee on Aging, United States Senate. Washington, DC: U.S. Government Printing Office.

Reemer, F. (1985, Spring). Facing up to the challenge of DRGs. *Health and Social Work, 10,* 85-94.

Rehr, H. (1984, Fall). Health care and social work services: Present concerns and future directions. *Social Work in Health Care, 10,* 71-83.

Rosenberg, G., & Rehr, H. (1983). *Advancing social work practice in the health care field.* New York: Haworth.

Wallace, S., Goldberg, R., & Slaby, A. (1984). *Clinical social work in health care.* New York: Praeger.

Chapter 3

THE GENERALIST'S ROLE

Kristine Siefert

INTRODUCTION

The variety and complexity of primary care settings and the diversity of demands made upon social workers practicing in primary care create a need for a versatile practice model. Schlesinger (1985) points out that primary care provides a unique opportunity to practice in a manner congruent with social work's traditional mandate to address both individual needs and deficits in the larger social environment. She also notes that such an approach can generate excitement and respect for the social worker's role. The generalist's approach, which requires that the social worker examine a problem from a broad perspective and be prepared to intervene at multiple levels in a range of situations, provides a suitable framework for such practice (Sheafor & Landon, 1987). This chapter describes the characteristics of the primary care setting, identifies key components of the generalist role, presents guidelines for establishing this role, and discusses a methodology for setting priorities. Subsequent chapters provide a more detailed examination of the specialized functions performed by social workers in various primary care settings.

PRIMARY CARE CHARACTERISTICS

Although definitions of primary care vary, certain generally agreed upon characteristics have significance for social work practice. Primary care is comprehensive, accessible, coordinated, continuous and accountable; it provides a continuum of services at each developmental stage throughout the life cycle (Miller, 1987). Primary care is a comprehensive care model in which providers are concerned with maintaining the health of the person or family as a whole, not just with treating an acute problem. Studies have demonstrated that patients who are experiencing social or emotional problems are more likely to turn to their family physicians than to a mental health practitioner. Many patients with emotional or psychiatric problems express physical symptoms for which there may or may not be an organic basis. In the latter situation, excessive and costly use of the health system can occur (Miller, 1987). Thus, assessment and intervention must address psychological, cultural and economic issues in addition to biological factors. Intervention should be directed to populations at risk and to individuals, and should be oriented to prevention, health promotion, and treatment.

Various organizations deliver primary care services. They range from simple forms such as individual for-profit medical practice to more complex forms such as prepaid health maintenance organizations, organized outpatient departments of hospitals, and federally funded programs such as community health centers, maternal and child health projects, and migrant health centers. Staffing patterns vary, but typically the patient has a specific physician who knows about the patient's history and who provides coordination of services through referral to other specialty health providers. Some primary care organizations employ only physicians representing basic medical specialties while others use a multidisciplinary team model representing a variety of health providers. Despite their differences, these settings have a common goal of bringing comprehensive, coordinated, continuous, and preventive care to a defined patient population from the point of first entry into the health care system. This requires that all providers be responsive to the full range of patient concerns and be able to address the "whole" person or family.

ESSENTIAL COMPONENTS: THE GENERALIST'S PERSPECTIVE

Primary care characteristics require a practice approach that considers the entire situation when making an assessment and when planning and implementing intervention. Assessment and goal-setting cannot be limited by the way a problem is initially presented, because the presenting problem in the primary care setting often is not the true problem, but rather one that has been medicalized (Ell & Morrison, 1981). Because health problems have multiple causes, intervention cannot be constrained by a worker's methodological bias. Ell and Morrison (1981) describe the primary care social worker as a generalist with broad knowledge. The generalist's approach to social work practice assumes that the worker has an eclectic theoretical base, uses a systems framework for assessment, is oriented to multilevel interventions, and takes responsibility for guiding the problem-solving or planned change process. The process includes intake and engagement, assessment, planning and contracting, intervention, monitoring and evaluation, and termination (Sheafor & Landon, 1987).

INTAKE, ENGAGEMENT, AND ASSESSMENT WITH PATIENTS AND FAMILIES

In these phases, the social worker contacts the patient or family, identifies the issues to be addressed, determines whether service can be provided or if referral to other services should be made, initiates the helping relationship, engages the patient in the planned change or problem-solving process, and collects and analyzes factual and impressionistic data concerning the patient and family systems and the other systems involved (Sheafor & Landon, 1987). The primary care setting and practice arrangements determine the access point for the patient's contact with the worker. In some settings, all new patients are referred to the social worker for psychological assessment. In other settings, patients are identified by social workers through the use of high-risk screening criteria, or they are referred to the social worker by physicians (Miller, 1987).

Using the epidemiologic concept of risk is critical to identifying patients and families who need social work intervention. Risk factors are biological, psychological, social, demographic or cultural characteristics that increase the vulnerability of a patient or population to various health or mental health problems. Table 3.1, "Maternal Medical, Reproductive, and Social Risk Factors," is an example of criteria that can be used in maternal and child health programs for identifying women at risk of miscarriages and other pregnancy difficulties. De-

Table 3.1

Maternal Medical, Reproductive, and Social Risk Factors

Medical and Reproductive Risk Factors
1. Chronic hypertension
2. Renal Disease
3. Diabetes mellitus
4. Cardiac disease
5. Cancer
6. Sickle-cell trait or disease
7. Anemia
8. Thyroid disorder
9. Gastrointestinal or liver disease
10. Epilepsy
11. Recurrent urinary tract infection
12. Nutritional deficiency
13. Mental retardation
14. Psychiatric disorder
15. Drug addiction, alcoholism or heavy smoking
16. Two or more spontaneous or induced abortions
17. Previous stillbirth or neonatal death
18. Previous premature delivery, low birth weight or intrauterine growth retardation
19. Previous excessively large infant
20. Fifth or greater pregnancy
21. Previous Rh isoimmunization
22. Preeclampsia-eclampsia
23. Previous infant with hereditary disorder or congenital anomaly
24. Previous infant birth-damaged or required neonatal intensive care
25. Family history of hereditary disorder
26. Maternal age under 18 or over 35

Social Risk Factors
1. Poverty
2. Substandard housing or environment
3. Lack of transportation
4. Less than high school education
5. Member of oppressed or underserved minority group
6. Single mother
7. Accidental or unwanted pregnancy
8. Adolescent pregnancy
9. Lack of experience in infant and child care
10. Social isolation
11. Stressful life event or conditions
12. Marital conflict
13. Family conflict
14. Previous history of child abuse or neglect
15. Drug or alcohol addiction

pending on the primary care setting, social risk criteria can be incorporated into the initial assessment of all new patients, can be used by the social worker for high-risk screening through record review, or can be used by the physician or other providers as the basis for referral to social work. Chapter 7, "Public Health Role," provides further information on casefinding and outreach. In addition to helping identify patients and families in need of service, risk factor screening can assist the social worker in determining whether she or he can provide the services needed, whether referral is indicated, and which issues should be addressed by social work intervention.

INFORMATION GATHERING AND ASSESSMENT AT THE COMMUNITY LEVEL

The clinical assessment of individual patients is described in detail in Chapter 4, "The Therapist's Role." In addition, the generalist social worker can contribute to primary care's goal of providing health promotion and disease prevention services by participating in community diagnosis and planning. This activity calls for assessment that is focused on the common needs and problems of the total patient population served by the primary care setting rather than on the unique characteristics of individual patients, which is the usual focus of clinical work. Using and contributing to the organization's data base is the first step in this process. Chapter 8, "Record Keeping and Data Collection," provides a detailed description of key data collection and management concepts and procedures.

Additional data may be needed to answer questions such as "Are there those in our population who are not being served? How many, and why?" Community diagnosis seeks to identify barriers to the overall health of the population served. Sources of information include vital statistics such as morbidity, mortality, fertility and disability; behavioral indicators such as usage, consumption patterns, compliance, self-care, and preventive actions; and subjectively defined community problems or social indicators such as unemployment, illegitimacy, welfare, discrimination, crime, and overcrowding (Green, Kreuter, Deeds, & Partridge, 1980). Some of the methods that can be used to identify social problems affecting health include literature reviews, the nominal group process, the Delphi method, a continuum approach, the use of key informants, and analysis of public service data (Green et al., 1980).

The problems revealed by such assessment may range from one's own programmatic and/or community service gaps to larger issues of socially structured deprivation and oppression. Such data have important implications for the development and implementation of health maintenance and preventive services. The primary care social worker can use them to develop or organize coalitions of concerned providers, consumers, and community leaders to translate the needs of the community into public policy, program goals, and program planning. A number of authors have noted that social workers in primary care have tended to emphasize a traditional clinical role. Consequently, the lack of consensus of social work's role in primary care and the need to demonstrate social work's importance have led to a neglect of the components of the primary care model that focus on policy and planning (Dana, 1983; Ell & Morrison, 1981; Schlesinger, 1985). Miller (1987) points out, however, that by participating in community health planning and policy formation, social workers contribute to primary care and promote other health providers' perception of social work as an essential service.

PLANNING, CONTRACTING, AND INTERVENING WITH PATIENTS AND FAMILIES

Once an assessment has been made and problems or risk factors have been identified, the generalist social worker, in consultation with the primary care physician and other relevant providers, considers with the patient or family the range of solutions available and the advantages and disadvantages of each; selects the most acceptable option; and develops a formal or informal contract designating responsibilities for each party involved. During intervention, each of the relevant systems carries out the agreed upon responsibility (Sheafor & Landon, 1987). Effective use of skills in consultation, discussed in detail in Chapter 6, and ongoing interdisciplinary collaboration, discussed in Chapter 9, are crucial to the successful planning and implementation of intervention. The continuous care responsibility of primary care does not mean that a single provider or program directly undertakes all activities necessary to resolve or ameliorate a patient's problems. It does mean that the primary care setting takes responsibility for ensuring that all of the various actions needed to accomplish the mutually agreed upon health care plan are taken. Time and technical capability are critical determinants of the nature and extent of the generalist social worker's involvement; thus, significant components of intervention are resource acquisition, referral, and advocacy.

The ability to link people with those particular sources of help appropriate to their needs is fundamental to all social work practice. In the clinical situation, a primary care user may require a variety of human services. The rapid growth in community services, increasing specialization, and changes in funding arrangements make resource acquisition and linkage a demanding task. Advocacy skills, described in Chapter 5, may be needed to engage an external organization's interest in serving a patient.

Another way in which social workers can promote resource acquisition is by using network strategies such as linking patients with self-help and mutual aid groups and generating resources within patients' existing social networks. For example, adult children and neighbors might be organized to identify a mutually agreeable contribution to a disabled person's well-being. In one such situation, a terminally ill cancer patient was able to remain at home rather than be placed in a nursing home. In this case, a social worker helped the patient's elderly husband ask a neighbor friend who was a retired nurse to assist with the injection of pain medication.

In addition to helping individual patients use existing resources, generalist social workers may seek to remedy resource deficits by changes in and additions to their own primary care programs. For example, one family practice setting observed the various health problems associated with spousal loss and initiated specific services directed to all their recently widowed persons who were using their other services. Primary care settings serving the poor often serve populations of cultural and ethnic diversity. Social workers can play an active role in developing programs that are sensitive to the health beliefs and behaviors of various ethnic groups (Schlesinger, 1985). Program consultation and advocacy skills can facilitate accomplishing such objectives. Expertise in linking patients with formal and informal community resources and in improving the content and quality of care in existing programs constitutes core generalist practice components. Creativity and innovation are also required if patients' needs are to be met.

COMMUNITY SERVICES DEVELOPMENT AND
SOCIAL POLICY CHANGE

The primary care social worker practicing from the generalist's perspective must go beyond clinical problem solving. Resource deficits become a concern in relation not only to those service users already requiring treatment or rehabilitation but also to those at risk. As noted earlier and discussed further in Chapters 7 and 8, social workers can use data collection systems to identify high-risk populations and to design and implement preventive interventions. In addition, the primary care social worker can identify community agencies accountable for specific high-risk populations, negotiate agreements between primary care programs and other programs, and advocate for needed services (Schlesinger, 1985). For example, a primary care social worker seeing substantial numbers of pregnant teens in a community where schools do not offer family life and sex education can initiate and/or join a community-based planning or advocacy group sharing this concern. The goal in such a situation would be to bring about comprehensive and effective school programs with potential for reducing the community-wide incidence of unintended teen pregnancy.

On a broader scale, social workers in primary care should be alert to patient problems that result from inadequate and inequitable public policy. Social workers should take the lead in building coalitions, setting policy, undertaking relevant research, and administering programs to resolve disparities in health status (Gitterman, Black & Stein, 1985). This requires using knowledge of macro levels of intervention to develop data, disseminate information, and influence public policy in addition to providing clinical services to overcome cultural and economic barriers to access and usage (Siefert, 1988).

The primary care social worker must understand general strategies for creating change: developing new information about a problem and making it available to those who need or are receptive to it; educating and stimulating the public; and using direct administrative or political power or control to change services, systems or programs (Torrens, 1978). Primary care social workers must know the basic steps required to carry out a strategy for change: accurately assess need, carefully establish objectives, obtain and review relevant and supportive data, and identify those people and groups with the power to accomplish change. The need for political action and advocacy has never been greater. Action to improve social conditions is part of the social worker's professional responsibility. Chapter 5, "The Advocate's Role," describes this social work practice role in primary care in more detail.

MONITORING AND EVALUATION

For the primary care social worker practicing from the generalist's perspective, monitoring and evaluation are conducted throughout the change process to ascertain the success of the planned intervention and the need for using other methods to achieve desired outcomes (Sheafor & Landon, 1987). In addition, interdisciplinary collaboration, as discussed in Chapter 9, permits monitoring of the patient's movement at every level of care (Miller, 1987). Intervention may be evaluated in terms of process, effect, and outcome.

Process evaluation monitors the acceptability or quality of practice. Effect evaluation focuses on the immediate effect of the intervention on the short-term goals of intervention. Outcome evaluation measures the long-term health and social benefits of intervention in terms of mortality, morbidity, and overall cost-effectiveness (Green, Kreuter, Deeds, & Partridge, 1980). Different designs may be used in evaluation, ranging from the collection of routine data on an ongoing basis to full-scale evaluative research projects. Chapter 8, "Record Keeping and Data Collection: Critical Elements for Quality Care," details some current methods for monitoring and evaluating social work practice in primary care.

DEFINING THE SOCIAL WORK ROLE AND SETTING PRIORITIES

Primary care social workers practice in a variety of settings that differ in locale, populations served, and major functions. Schlesinger (1985) points out, however, that certain features are characteristic of social work practice in any health care setting:

- social work services are often viewed as ancillary to the major function of the setting;
- patients often are present in a crisis situation;
- settings are complex organizations;
- when specialized services are offered, most providers must develop relevant expertise;

- when a diverse population is served, most workers need to become familiar with a variety of physical and mental disorders;
- opportunities for prevention and health promotion must be recognized and used when health care is delivered as part of another service system such as the workplace or school;
- outreach and health planning require knowledge of community health problems and priorities.

Thus, it is critical that primary care social workers be aware of the organizational structure and major functions of the setting; the recurrent medical, psychological, and social problems seen; the community, current health, and social policy developments and regulations; and their own areas of expertise and limitations (Schlesinger, 1985).

Optimally, the social work role is defined and a social service plan is established before or within the first two weeks of employment. The plan should be based upon criteria that have been mutually agreed upon by the employer, providers, and worker. No single social worker can meet the needs of all patients, providers, and administrators, but if expectations are clarified and priorities are set, dissatisfaction and conflicts that could detract from patient care can be minimized.

The first step in setting priorities for social work activities is to assess the significant health and psychosocial needs of the patient population served. This can be done by using existing practice data (see Chapter 8) or by administering patient and/or provider questionnaires.

The second step is to meet with administrators and determine their goals in light of the problems that have been identified through assessment of patient needs. It is essential that the primary care social worker have a clear understanding of the needs and expectations of the setting to determine the extent to which each aspect of the generalist role should be used. If generating revenue through providing clinical services reimbursed by third-party payments or patient fees is a priority for the setting, for instance, the therapist's role is likely to be emphasized. If developing programs for high-risk patients is a priority, the public health role is most appropriate. In other settings, advocacy may be the major social work activity.

In a primary care setting in which it is left up to the social worker to define his or her role and there are insufficient staff to meet patient needs, the following strategies should be considered:

First, attempt to train physicians and other providers to make their own referrals to social service agencies. Some of the ways in which this can be accomplished are by providing in-service training, holding joint conferences, and developing an information and referral booklet. Chapter 6, "The Consultant's Role," and Chapter 9, "Interprofessional Collaboration," provide further information.

Second, whenever possible, integrate categorical community-based services into the primary care system. For example, could the WIC food program for mothers and infants be provided on-site? Could a child guidance clinic or community mental health center provide staff to see patients in the primary care setting? Centralizing services promotes patient access and maximizes scarce resources.

Finally, patients should be referred to existing resources whenever possible rather than developing new services. This avoids expensive and inefficient duplication.

SUMMARY

This chapter has described the mission and characteristics of primary care. It presents the generalist's approach to social work practice, which is characterized by broad-based assessment and intervention at multiple levels, and is sufficiently comprehensive and versatile to meet the demands of social workers in primary care settings. Since no single social work role is sufficient to meet the needs of all primary care patients, guidelines for setting priorities and maximizing resources are suggested.

REFERENCES

Dana, B. (1983). Collaboration in primary care, or is it? In R. S. Miller (Ed.), *Primary health care: More than medicine*. Englewood Cliffs, NJ: Prentice-Hall.

Ell, K., & Morrison, D. R. (1981). Primary care. *Health and Social Work, 6*(4), Supplement, 35S-48S.

Gitterman, A., Black, R., & Stein, F. (1985). *Public health social work in maternal and child health: A forward plan*. Rockville, MD: Maternal and Child Health, U.S. Department of Health and Human Services.

Green, L. W., Kreuter, M. W., Deeds, S. G., & Partridge, K. B. (1980). *Health education planning: A diagnostic approach*. Palo Alto, CA: Mayfield.

Miller, R. S. (1987). Primary health care. *Encyclopedia of social work*. Silver Spring, MD: National Association of Social Workers.

Schlesinger, E. G. (1985). *Health care social work practice: Concepts and strategies*. St. Louis, MO: Times Mirror/Mosby.

Sheafor, B. W., & Landon, P. S. (1987). Generalist perspective. *Encyclopedia of social work*. Silver Spring, MD: National Association of Social Workers.

Siefert, K. (1985). Identifying mothers at medical and social risk. In D. Rodman & A. Murphy (Eds.), *Perinatal care in the '80's: Social work strategies for prevention and intervention.* Rockville, MD: Maternal and Child Health, U.S. Department of Health and Human Services.

Siefert, K. (1988). Disparity in birth outcomes: Implications for public health social work. In J. Morton (Ed.), *Advocacy and outreach: Developing social work programs to prevent low birthweight and infant mortality.* Rockville, MD: Maternal and Child Health, U.S. Department of Health and Human Services.

Torrens, P. (1978). *The American health care system: Issues and problems.* St. Louis, MO: Mosby.

Chapter 4

THE THERAPIST'S ROLE

William H. Butterfield

Medical social workers traditionally have practiced in hospitals and other acute care health settings. Unfortunately, this type of practice limits the scope of treatment services because most patient problems cannot be resolved during hospitalization. Furthermore, caseloads are often excessive and the patient population transient. Hospital-based social workers usually function in an advocacy and brokerage role and engage in case finding, referral, and counseling of patients. Counseling is usually limited to brief supportive therapy and finding needed resources for patients. As hospital outpatient services become more available and more comprehensive, social workers must adapt to provide more of the services described in this chapter. In addition, social workers have moved into primary care settings where the patient is treated for both medical and psychosocial problems that usually do not require hospitalization. Primary care settings tend to have a less transient patient population and a significant number of patients with mental health problems; therefore, a new model of social work practice must be developed in which the emphasis changes from case manager to therapist.

Psychosocial problems cannot be managed through referrals alone. Kaeser and Cooper (1971) found that about 50% of referrals to mental health facilities were unsuccessful. Sue, McKinney, and Allen (1976) report similar findings. They found that 40% to 50% of referred patients failed to appear for a second interview at a community mental health center. Kaeser and Cooper (1971) found that only 42% of referred patients reported an improvement in the problem for which they were referred.

Social workers functioning in the therapist role will have primary treatment responsibility for the following types of problems:

1. Social and interpersonal.
2. Emotional or other "mental" problems that interfere with the client's ability to function.
3. Anxiety and other problems in which the patient worries about real or imagined medical problems that do not merit medical intervention. Clients with these types of problems are sometimes called the "worried well" (Rher, 1983).
4. Failure to comply with medical regimens.

Estimates vary as to the extent of these problems in primary care settings. They range from about 9% (Kessel, 1965) to about 20% (Kellner, 1966). Because both authors appear to exclude the worried well, incidence of these problems could be much higher. L. Thomas (1977), for example, estimates that almost 75% of medical visits to primary care providers are for problems that do not involve physical disease. A recent article regarding a large health maintenance organization (HMO) in Kansas City, Missouri pointed out that 85,000 enrollees generated 23,000 mental health visits during a one-year period (*Kansas City Times*, September 20, 1988).

To develop an effective mental health treatment model, physicians and nurses must transfer primary responsibility for social and interpersonal problems, medical compliance problems, and emotional and psychological problems to the social worker. Although many primary care settings justifiably place a major emphasis on the therapist role, it should be viewed in the overall context of social worker roles. Other roles discussed in this book should be integrated into primary care social work practice whenever possible.

Social workers under the present systems of reimbursement cannot generate the same levels of revenue as do physicians or psychologists who deliver similar services (Hookey, 1978). Although this is the case, many primary care settings are willing to accept the lower revenues because social work services improve the scope and quality of patient care. Social workers often provide definitive care for problems that physicians, and to a lesser extent nurses and psychologists, are not equipped to handle. They also free up medical staff time that might otherwise be spent dealing with the worried well and patients with emotional and psychological problems. Many doctors have found that it makes economic sense to refer these patients to a social worker. The inclusion of social work services in the primary care setting allows comprehensive care to be delivered that is both economical and valued by patients. While a more comprehensive service model might be professionally desirable, the need to recover costs and generate income may force primary care settings to use the mental health or service model. Publicly funded primary care settings offer more services than do large for-profit group practices because costs of some social work services can be written off as overhead. Social work services in primary care settings must be as efficient and effective as possible to minimize costs, maximize income, and reduce the amount of time the patient spends in the clinic (Nooe, 1976).

The following section discusses a practice model that has been successfully used in primary care settings (Brockway, Werking, Fitzgibbons, & Butterfield, 1976; Butterfield & Parson, 1973; Butterfield & Werking, 1981). Similar models can be found in many outpatient behavioral medicine clinics (Redd & Rusch, 1985). The model assumes that treatment should focus on "increasing people's own competencies so that they will be able to enhance the quality of their lives both currently and in the future" (Gambrill, 1983).

This model also assumes that if clients are to become more competent they must learn new ways of behaving and thinking. To accomplish this therapists must be effective teachers. Not only are effective therapists supportive, but they also motivate patients and help them reduce anxiety, and remain optimistic about the outcome of a patient's treatment. In their roles as teachers and therapists social workers:

1. Provide patients with knowledge about the problem being treated.
2. Teach patients to view their problems from different perspectives.
3. Teach patients to be problem solvers.
4. Teach patients new skills and behaviors.
5. Teach patients to set specific, attainable goals that focus on the problem, are limited in time, and that define outcomes from the patient's perspective rather than the social worker's perspective (Donabedian, 1966).
6. Teach patients to evaluate their own outcomes and progress.
7. Collaborate with patients in developing and implementing intervention plans.
8. Set expectations that patients are responsible for their own treatment and progress.

Several authors have written texts that discuss similar treatment models (see Cormier & Cormier, 1985; Gambrill, 1983; Miller & Rher, 1983; and E. J. Thomas, 1984).

IDENTIFYING PATIENTS

The first step in the intervention process is patient identification or case finding. In primary care settings the first professional to see the client is usually a nurse or a nurse's aide. Next the patient is likely to see a physician or a physician's assistant. Because the effectiveness of the social work service depends largely on how these professionals evaluate patient needs, the social worker must teach the other staff members how to identify and refer patients appropriately. Some of the most commonly used methods of patient identification and staff instruction include:

1. Using screening instruments such as check lists or questionnaires that are completed by patients. The results can then be shared with professional staff, and appropriate referrals identified. See Berkman, Rher, and Rosenberg (1980) for an example of a screening instrument.
2. Developing a list of stressful life situations that can be used by staff to identify patients who may be at risk. Some practices have used the Holmes-Rahe (1967) Stress Index for this purpose.
3. Teaching staff to use open-ended questions and other interviewing techniques to gather information (Engle & Morgan, 1973).
4. Encouraging staff to use the Problem-Oriented Record to record patient contacts (Ruback, Longabaugh & Fowler, 1981).
5. Accompanying physicians in their rounds or sitting in on office visits with patients.
6. Volunteering to work with particularly problematic patients who have problems appropriate for social work intervention. Typical difficult patients are those who fear or resist health care and are noncompliant. Almost two-thirds of primary care patients do not fully comply with health plans (Davis, 1966). Social work is beginning to develop ways to address these problems (Shelton & Levy, 1981).

PATIENT SELECTION

The medical concept of triage is essential to the patient identification process. There are more patient problems than can be effectively treated by the primary care staff. Some problems are best left untreated while others can be delayed. Still others require immediate attention. Priorities must be established and decisions made about which patients should receive services.

Several criteria have been suggested:

1. Chronic versus acute problems. Chronic problems are of long duration, and they may be severe or benign. Acute problems have a sudden onset or an abrupt increase in severity. Acute problems are more likely to be seen as crises. Because there is substantial evidence that people in crisis are much more receptive to change, working with people in crisis may be highly beneficial.

2. Public versus private problems. Behavior that harms others or that offends public sensibilities is more likely to require immediate attention. This includes problems that are highly annoying to the medical staff or that interfere with medical treatment.

3. Ability to function. Chronic or acute problems can mildly or severely disrupt the day-to-day functioning of patients. The disruption may be either long-term or short-term. some patients may improve without intervention. Immediate attention is usually warranted, however, for acute problems that severely disrupt a person's day-to-day functioning or where the danger of these problems becoming chronic is high.

4. Availability of support networks. Most patients have many sources of help and support, but some do not. Isolated patients generally need more immediate attention.

5. The probability of success. Some problems are quickly and easily treated, but others require long-term intervention or heroic efforts and massive allocations of resources. Where the former problems are not trivial, they probably should take precedence over the largely untreatable problems.

Although these categories are not mutually exclusive nor exhaustive, they do provide guidelines for the health care team in determining those patients to refer and those to defer. The process of client identification and problem identification is closely linked and iterative. The first screening determines who is referred for service. Subsequent screenings refine the first assessment and lead to the development of a contract to help a patient with a specific problem.

PROBLEM IDENTIFICATION

The development of agreements to work on specific problems begins with problem identification. This involves the collection of relevant information for the purpose of generating a list of problems. E. J. Thomas (1984) refers to this process as developing an inventory of problem areas. The process begins by identifying general problem areas and is refined until specific problems are identified. Information about the specific problems is then used to plan interventions and evaluation. In the problem identification stage, the worker collects enough information so that problems can be labeled. This stage does not involve an in-depth examination of the problem. At this stage the worker is interested simply in ascertaining that the problem exists and needs to be added to the problem list.

The next step is prioritization, where the criteria we discussed earlier are used to decide which problems to examine in depth. This approach does not assume that it is necessary to know all about a problem before proceeding to establish treatment priorities. It does assume that as more information is developed, the problem priorities may be modified.

PROBLEM SPECIFICATION

Once the problem has been selected, the next task is specification, which is to develop enough information to treat the problem successfully. Specification varies with the problem domain, but includes the following:

1. Developing clear objectives that
   a. Are stated in positive terms and build on patient assets.
   b. Are attainable.
   c. Specify who will do what under what circumstances and when.
   d. Focus on behavior or environmental change rather than on indirect effects of change.
   e. Include intermediate steps.
   f. Avoid confusion between outcomes and process.
   g. Include easy-to-use measures for assessing progress toward objectives.
2. Offering the patient control in achieving the desired change.
3. Addressing patient concerns so that objectives are meaningful and relevant.
4. Assuring that immediate and long-term benefits accrue to patients, but do not lead to undesirable consequences for others.

5. Developing explicit agreements with the patient and significant others to pursue the objectives.

6. Specified objectives should represent the most effective method available to solve the problem. (Gambrill, 1983)

This type of specification differs from traditional social work assessment procedures. In this context, information gathering and specification are limited to collecting only that information directly and immediately applicable to the resolution of the present problem. Specification is an interactive process in which the patient, the therapist, and others exchange information and arrive at a mutually agreed on set of goals and procedures.

Specification also differs from traditional medical diagnosis. Medical diagnosis is a categorization process used to identify specific illnesses or disease processes. This information is then used to develop specific medical interventions. Although medical diagnosis is similar to problem identification, the latter approach does not assume that all problems are diseases or illnesses or that they can be properly categorized using traditional medical diagnostic categories. Some social workers will have to use medical diagnostic codes because of governmental or insurance regulations, but this practice should be avoided whenever possible.

There are sound legal and professional reasons for avoiding the use of medical diagnostic categories. A recent article by Kutchins and Kirk (1987) discusses this issue. Although medical diagnosis should be avoided, it is nevertheless essential to classify and record psychosocial problems in a problem-oriented manner (see Chapter 8).

INTERVENTION

Problems are best solved in the setting in which they occur. The evidence to support this view is compelling (Gambrill, 1983, 1977; Lutzker & Rice, 1984; Shelton & Levy, 1981). When patients deal with problems in their normal environments and when the issue of the maintenance of treatment gains are specifically addressed, the probability of long-term improvement increases.

Most interventions require the involvement of more than one or two people and the use of the multiple procedures. The social worker is responsible for some actions and the patient for others. In many cases additional activities must be carried out by others.

The majority of interventions take place outside the therapist's office. When the social worker and the patient do meet, they should focus on:

1. Monitoring and evaluation of progress.
2. Clarifying issues.
3. Setting new goals.
4. Assigning tasks and identifying means to accomplish them.
5. Rehearsing the tasks and practicing the skills the patient needs to accomplish the goals.
6. Acquiring new knowledge and skills and clarifying patient's concerns and perceptions.

Implementing the intervention plan requires monitoring, planning, patient education, and evaluation.

The monitoring process. Although the specific procedures used vary with the type of problem being treated, the following activities are needed to structure the monitoring process.

1. Obtaining commitment from patient to monitor progress.
2. Establishing minimal monitoring demands and increasing them over time.
3. Providing explicit instructions that answer the following questions:
   a. What is to be measured or observed and by whom?
   b. What consultants and outside resources will be contacted and what will be requested of them?
   c. What will be recorded and by what method?
   d. How will it be recorded?
   e. Where will the recording device or instrument be kept?
   f. Who will have access to the device or instrument?
   g. Who should be contacted if difficulties or questions about monitoring occur?
4. Requesting that the patient discuss his understanding of how each of the above items will be accomplished.
5. Encouraging the patient to role play the desired behaviors.

The patient education process. Patient education is essential to treatment. A major role of the therapist is to teach patients new ways to act and think and to modify their environments. Teaching provides information that gives the patient new ways of looking at old problems.

Although patients have many skills and competencies, the therapist should not assume those skills exist until the patient has been able to demonstrate them successfully to the therapist. Furthermore, it is important to remember that some skills are situation specific. If a patient has difficulties in carrying out assignments, training may have to be moved into the patient's normal living environment.

A few examples may help to clarify these points. If a patient needs to learn how to be assertive with people who make unreasonable demands, the worker should check to see if the patient has a repertoire of assertive responses, and have the patient simulate the conversations while still in the therapist's office. The coaching should continue until there is a high probability that the patient will have success in the natural environment. Finally, the worker might want to be present when the patient first tries the new assertive behavior.

A couple trying to develop better communication might first review the goals they want to accomplish and then practice the communication until they feel able to carry it out on their own. A patient who needs to control his anxiety might first learn how to relax in the therapist's office and only later apply those skills in less controlled settings.

Skills are developed through practice. Gambrill (1983) suggests several criteria for evaluating whether patients understand and can learn new skills. They include:

1. The goals are specific.
2. The assignment will be useful to participants.
3. The rationale for the assignment has been explained.
4. The person is capable of carrying out the task.
5. The person can correctly describe what is to be done, where and when it is to be done, and the rationale for carrying out the task.
6. The worker has demonstrated how to carry out the assignment.
7. Opportunities to carry out the assignment are available in the patient's environment.
8. The assignment is strength-oriented: that is, focused largely on positive behaviors, feelings, thoughts, or environmental characteristics.
9. Positive incentives have been arranged for carrying out the assignment.
10. Helpful forms or electro-mechanical devices (such as a wrist counter or tape recorder) that will make the task easier have been provided.
11. Possible problems in carrying out the assignment have been anticipated.
12. The assignment is not overly intrusive.
13. The assignment will not have negative effects.

14. A specific time to review the results has been set.

15. They will result in positive outcomes in real-life settings.

The evaluation process. In the model just proposed, evaluation takes place continuously. Each time the worker and patient meet, talk to each other on the phone, or exchange written communication, the worker needs to review the data generated by the monitoring process to determine whether tasks have been accomplished and whether treatment goals are being met. When evaluation shows that the intervention plan is not on schedule, the worker and the patient must alter the plan or the tasks needed to produce continued progress. Evaluation is ongoing, interactive, and integral to the treatment process.

The clinical techniques used by the therapist in primary care settings differ little from the techniques used in other settings where similar problems are treated. Nevertheless, as is pointed out elsewhere in this book, when taken as a whole, the types of services a social worker may provide are more varied and are more closely integrated into the overall care a patient is receiving.

A short composite example may make the differences clearer. A patient referred herself because she was having severe jaw pain. The assessment process established that in addition to jaw pain, the patient was failing to maintain weight and was experiencing social isolation, nightmares, and high levels of personal and job-related stress.

Before treating the jaw pain and weight loss, the social worker arranged for the problems to be medically evaluated. In this case the medical assessment established that no underlying organic disease processes were contributing to the problems. The social worker then developed a comprehensive treatment plan including biofeedback training for the reduction of the jaw pain, relaxation training for stress reduction, and social skills development for the reduction of the patient's social isolation.

Concurrently, the nutritionist worked with the patient on the weight loss problem. The physician and the social worker worked together to help the patient deal with the jaw pain. The physician prescribed medication to relieve the pain and as the patient progressed, reduced the medication to levels consistent with the biofeedback treatment the patient was receiving. The social worker served as the case manager and the primary point of contact for the patient. Weekly progress notes were prepared by each staff person seeing the patient. The social worker then prepared a weekly summary for the staff and, as necessary, called staff conferences to plan the next stages of the patient's treatment program.

Throughout this process, the procedures and techniques outlined earlier were used to guide planning and treatment. The treatment was problem-focused but multifaceted. A formal treatment plan was developed and implemented for each of the identified problems. As necessary, medical personnel were involved in diagnosis and treatment. The social worker was responsible for ensuring that key staff were informed, monitored the patient on each of the identified problems, and made sure that the patient and staff efforts were coordinated. The care the patient received was integrated and built on the expertise of several health professionals. The fact that all the services were integrated and that each plan for each problem was followed is what makes social work services in primary care settings so useful and desirable and what distinguishes this type of care from similar treatments offered in other settings.

SUMMARY

This chapter has outlined some of the realities of social work practice in primary care settings and has proposed a time-limited problem-focused model of practice designed to meet these constraints. Although the model has general application, it is particularly appropriate for social workers whose prime focus is on patients with emotional and family problems. Social workers who focus in this area are essentially mental health therapists working in a primary care setting. This role should prove to be challenging, interesting and well-suited to primary care settings.

REFERENCES

Berkman, B., Rher, H., & Rosenberg, G. (1980). A social work department creates and tests a screening mechanism to identify high social risk. *Social Work in Health Care*, 5(4), 373-385.

Brockway, B., Werking, J., Fitzgibbons, K., & Butterfield, W. (1976). Social work in the doctor's office. In B. Ross and S. Khinduka (Eds.) *Social work in practice*. Washington, DC: National Association of Social Workers.

Butterfield, W., & Parson, R. (1973). Modeling and shaping by parents to develop chewing behavior in their retarded child. *Journal of Behavior Therapy & Experimental Psychiatry, 4*, 295-287.

Butterfield, W., & Werking, J. (1981). Behavioral intervention with health problems. In
    S. Schinke (Ed.), *Community application of behavioral methods: A source book for
    social workers* (pp. 287-302). Chicago, IL: Aldine.

Cormier, W.H., & Cormier, L. S. (1985). *Interviewing strategies for helpers* (2nd ed.).
    Belmont, CA: Brooks/Cole.

Davis, M.S. (1966). Variations in patient compliance with doctor's orders: Analysis of
    congruence between survey responses and results of empirical investigators. *Journal
    of Medical Education, 41*(11), 1037-1048.

Donabedian, A. (1966, Spring). Evaluating the quality of medical care. *The Milbank
    Memorial Fund Quarterly, 4*, 166-203.

Engle, G., & Morgan, W. (1973). *Interviewing the patient.* London: W.B. Saunders.

Gambrill, E. (1983). *Casework: A competency based approach.* Englewood Cliffs, NJ:
    Prentice-Hall.

Holmes, T., & Rahe, R. (1967). The social readjustment rating scale. *Journal of Psycho-
    somatic Research, 11*, 213-218.

Hookey, P. (1978). Social work in primary health settings. In N. F. Bracht (Ed.), *Social
    work in health care: A guide to professional practice* (pp. 211-223). New York:
    Haworth Press.

Kaeser, A., & Cooper, B. (1971). The psychiatric patient, the general practitioner and the
    outpatient clinic: An operational study and a review. *Psychological Medicine, 1*,
    312-325.

Kellner, R. (1966). Neurotic symptoms in women: Attendance in a general practice.
    British Journal of Psychiatry, 112, 75-77.

Kessel, N. (1965). The neurotic in general practice. *The Practitioner, 194*, 636-641.

Kutchins, H., & Kirk, S. (1987). DSM-III and social work malpractice. *Social Work,
    32*(3), 205-211.

Lutzker, J., & Rice, J. (1984). Project 12-ways: Measuring outcome of a large in-home
    service for the treatment and prevention of child abuse and neglect. *Child Abuse and
    Neglect, 8*, 519-524.

Miller, R.S., & Rher, H. (Eds.). (1983). *Social work issues in health care.* Englewood
    Cliffs, NJ: Prentice-Hall.

Nooe, R. (1976). A clinical model for rural practice. In R. Green & S. Webster (Eds.),
    Social work in rural areas (pp. 347-360). Knoxville: The University of Tennessee.

Redd, W.H., & Rusch, F.R. (1985). Behavioral analysis in behavioral medicine. *Behavior
    Modification, 9*(2), 131-154.

Rher, H. (1983). The consumer and consumerism. In R.S. Miller & H. Rher (Eds.), *Social
    work issues in health care.* Englewood Cliffs, NJ: Prentice-Hall.

Ruback, R., Longabaugh, R., & Fowler, R. (1981). *The problem oriented record in
    psychiatry and mental health.* New York: Grune & Stratton.

Shelton, J. L., & Levy, R. L. (1981). *Behavioral assignments and treatment compliance:
    A handbook of clinical strategies.* Champaign, IL: Research Press.

Sue, S., McKinney, H. L., & Allen, D. B. (1976). Predictors of duration of therapy for
    clients in the community health center system. *Community Mental Health Journal,
    Vol 12*(4), 367-375.

Thomas, E.J. (1984). *Designing interventions for the helping professions.* Beverly Hills,
    CA: Sage.

Thomas, L. (1977). On the science and technology of medicine. *Daedalus, 6*(1), 42.

FURTHER READING

American Psychiatric Association. (1980). *Diagnostic and statistical manual of mental disorders* (3rd ed.). Washington, DC: Author.

Barone, V., Green, B., & Lutzker, J. (1986). Home safety with families being treated for child abuse and neglect. *Behavior Modification, 10*(1), 93-114.

Bergman, A., Dassel, S., & Wedgewood, R. (1966). Time motion study of practicing pediatricians. *Pediatrics, 38,* 254.

Bloom, M., & Fischer, J. (1982). *Evaluating practice: Guidelines for the accountable professional.* Englewood Cliffs, NJ: Prentice-Hall.

Bracht, N.F. (1978). *Social work in health care: A guide to professional practice.* New York: Haworth.

Bulau, J.M. (1986). *Administrative policies for home health.* Fredrick, MD: Aspen Systems.

Clare, A.W., & Corney, R.H. (Eds.). (1982). *Social work and primary health care.* London: Academic Press.

Farley, O. W., Griffiths, K.A., Skidmore, R.A., & Thalkeray, M.G. (1982). *Rural social work practice.* New York: Free Press.

Fassler, D. (1985). The fear of needles in children. *American Journal of Orthopsychiatry, 55*(3), 371-377.

Frentz, C., & Kelly, M.L. (1986). Parents' acceptance of reductive treatment methods: The influence of problem severity and perception of child behavior. *Behavior Therapy, 17*(1), 75-81.

Gambrill, E. (1977). *Behavior modification handbook of assessment intervention and evaluation.* San Francisco: Jossey-Bass.

Goldberg, D., & Blackwell, B. (1970). Psychiatric illness in general practice: A detailed study using the method of case identification. *British Medical Journal, 2,* 439-443.

Gurin, G., Veroff, J., & Feld, S. (1960). *Americans view their mental health.* New York: Basic Books.

Hankin, J., & Oktay, J. (1979). *Mental disorder and primary medical care: An analytical review of the literature.* Washington, D.C.: U.S. Department of Health, Education and Welfare.

Hartmann, D., Roper, B., & Bradford, D. (1979). Some relationships between behavioral and traditional assessment. *Journal of Behavioral Assessment, 1*(1), 3-21.

Heaster, W., (1988, September 20). *Kansas City Times,* Kansas, MO.

Kazdin, A.E. (1985). Selection of target behaviors: The relationship of treatment focus to clinical dysfunction. *Behavioral Assessment, 7*(1), 33-27.

Kirkland, K. (1981). Type of referrals to a behavior therapist in a family practice center. *Behavior Therapist, 4*(3), 15-16.

Koles, M.R. (1985). Comprehensive treatment of chronic fire setting in a severely disordered boy. *Journal of Behavior Therapy and Experimental Psychiatry, 16*(1), 81-85.

Kowalski, R. (1985). *Brief behavioral psychotherapy with psychosocial handbook of assessment intervention and evaluation.* San Francisco: Jossey-Bass.

Kumabe, K., Nishida, C., O'Hara, D., & Woodruff, C. (1977). *A handbook for social work education and practice in community health settings.* Honolulu: School of Social Work, University of Hawaii.

Lechnyr, R. (1984). Clinical social work psychotherapy and insurance coverage: Information on billing procedures. *Clinical Social Work Journal, 12*(1), 67-77.

Nay, W.R. (1979). *Multi-method clinical assessment.* New York: Gardner.

Robinson, S.E., & Stiefel, S. (1985). Familiar techniques with new applications: Counselling cancer patients. *Journal of Counselling and Development, 64*(1), 81-83.

Sergis, D.E., & Varni, J.W. (1983). Behavioral assessment: A management of adherence to factor replacement therapy in hemophilia. *Journal of Pediatric Psychology, 8*(4), 367-377.

Shader, R.I., & Greenblat, D.J. (1983). Some current treatment opinions for symptoms of anxiety. *Journal of Clinical Psychiatry, 44*(11), 21-29.

Starfield, B., & Borkowf, S. (1969). Physician recognition of complaints made by parents about their children's health. *Pediatrics, 43*, 170.

Stone, M. (1978). PSRO: Implication for social work participation in rural health care delivery work. *Social Welfare in Appalachia, 10*, 25-28.

Vernon, L.J., & Best, C.L. (1983). Assessment and treatment of rape-induced fear and anxiety. *Clinical Psychologist, 36*(4), 99-101.

Walsh, M. (1981). Rural social work practice: Clinical quality. *Social Casework, 62*, 458-464.

Whitehead, W.E., & Bosmajian, B.S. (1982). Behavioral medicine approaches to gastrointestinal disorders. *Journal of Consulting and Clinical Psychology, 50*(6), 972-983.

Chapter 5

THE ADVOCATE'S ROLE

Jane Collins

Physicians and administrators historically have associated social work services with advocacy functions. Although this misconception may limit the range of services that social workers can provide in a primary care setting, it can be viewed as a necessary first step in establishing a role within the health team while also providing an essential service for the patients.

Chapter 11 discusses how this attitude evolved and Chapter 10 discusses why administrators view advocacy as an important service. The reasons the advocacy role is frequently used before all others include:

1. Economic issues require that patients be able to pay for services. These funds will in turn pay for staff and other operational costs. That a social work department is able to produce more sources of payment than the cost of such a department can be justified on historic grounds.
2. Time, knowledge, and role constraints prohibit physicians and nurses from assuming this responsibility. Time given to psychosocial problems reduces revenue because these services are not usually covered by third party sources.
3. Patient needs require that social services be available. This type of service supports the avowed purpose of the setting: that is, to provide comprehensive care.

Advocacy as it is used in this chapter is divided into three components. The first is that activity that ensures that appropriate care and resources are provided or are developed for individual patients, families, or a group of patients in accordance with accepted standards of care. The second component discusses interprofessional collaboration. The third component is the function of advocating on behalf of specific groups or individual patients and program development.

In each of the three components, there may be either case advocacy or class advocacy. In case advocacy, the social worker " . . . gives primacy to the interests of individual clients" (Encyclopedia of Social Work, 1987). Class advocacy involves the social worker's action on behalf of a group of persons who share the same problem(s).

Most social workers in a primary care setting will engage in more case advocacy than class advocacy by the nature of their jobs, which are usually individual patient or family focused. Opportunities for class advocacy may occur when the social worker provides governmental or private agencies with data so they can develop or improve programs. Other opportunities for class advocacy can be the outcome of activities of professional, special interest, or political organizations.

Brokerage and advocacy are identified as separate activities. Brokerage is determining that those services which are required by a patient are provided for the necessary period of time. Advocacy involves the development of needed services or activities that ensure that the rights of patients are respected.

Physicians and nurses view the social worker as the person who is both knowledgeable of community and financial resources and skillful in assessing patient needs. The social worker not only needs to determine the resources which the patient may be eligible to use but also must be an advocate to help the patient approach the identified resources with correct expectations. Although some social workers regard providing referral service for financial assistance and other resources as denigrating to their roles as professionals, most understand that it is part of the therapeutic process. It is important that agencies be given sufficient information so that they will accept the referral, that eligibility requirements be fully understood, and that counseling be provided to patients so that they do not feel demeaned by the referral and understand the services to which they are being referred.

Helping patients to obtain home health care services, medical equipment, legal services or income maintenance services is crucial to the patient's ability to function in his/her own setting.

THE REFERRAL PROCESS

The major programs to which referrals are made include entitlement programs, insurance programs, training programs, long-term and alternative care programs, counseling services, and legal services. The nature of the institutional setting determines those agencies to which referrals are most frequently made.

The entitlement programs include those that are publicly funded and are available to those persons who are eligible under specific income, resource, age, and (when applicable) residence guidelines. Examples of entitlement programs are Supplemental Security Income (SSI), Medicaid, Aid to Families with Dependent Children (AFDC), Aid to the Blind, Aid to the Needy Disabled, and State Handicapped Children's Programs.

The social worker making referrals to the entitlement programs must understand the specific eligibility requirements of each agency to accomplish health care plans and to avoid unnecessary or inappropriate referrals that may reinforce the patient's negative self-image. In order to be current with the type and range of services each agency provides, the social worker must meet frequently with key agency staff and participate in community meetings and on committees and boards.

Legislation at both the federal and state levels frequently changes eligibility requirements and funding amounts for the entitlement programs. DEFRA (the Deficit Expenditure Fiscal Responsibility Act) and COBRA (Consolidated Omnibus Budget Reconciliation Act of 1985) are examples of such changes implemented by State Medicaid programs. Social workers who identify children in a family who appear to be eligible for one of the mandated Medicaid programs may need to explain their interpretation of the legislation to a Social Services (Public Assistance Department) technician or intake staff person so that all eligibility considerations will be noted.

It is particularly important for a social worker in primary care to be current on entitlement programs because patients' conditions or illnesses can be a determining factor in eligibility. A pregnant woman may be eligible for Medicaid for only a limited period of time, but that insurance coverage may be crucial to her or her family's financial situation during the months of her pregnancy. Counseling to help parents use ongoing treatment for their child under a Handicapped Children's Program may mean the difference between comprehensive curative treatment and episodic or discontinued care.

Although Social Security's disability, retirement, and Medicare programs provide essential services to the elderly, some patients will not be able to take full advantage of such services. Some patients will need help in working through their negative feelings of dependency before they are willing to apply for Medicare or for the SSI for which they may be eligible.

Patients who appear to be eligible for vocational rehabilitation or sheltered workshop training programs often do not follow through with referrals. The resistances held by the patient are often complex and based on patterns of behavior that have developed over years. The psychological satisfactions found in dependency and illness are often difficult and frightening to give up. The social worker should anticipate that it may take weeks or months of counseling before a patient will contact the rehabilitation agency. Even at that point, the case should be kept open because there is often the need to continue to support the patient in expressing and dealing with his/her resistance after he/she has initiated contact and begun a training program.

Many training and employment programs have regular meetings to report on the patient's progress and to identify methods of resolving problems presented by the patient. If social workers can remain active in the case, at least in the initial months, their input to the staff can be supportive of the patient. It is essential that the primary care setting obtain feedback on the progress of the patient so that the health care and training plans can be mutually supportive and, when appropriate, modified.

Patients with varying levels and types of disabilities need assistance placement away from home or with home health care services. A satisfactory placement takes into consideration both the needs and functional ability of the patient and what the setting can offer him or her. The social worker must have knowledge not only of the setting but also of the rules and regulations that determine eligibility for reimbursement to the facility or for care at home. Often reimbursement from more than one agency is used to achieve home health care coverage.

Community mental health and developmentally disabled services are other programs that are frequently used. Again, close follow-up on referrals is essential to achieve desired outcomes. Patients may need preparatory counseling before they are willing to accept referrals, particularly for mental health services. Patients fear that they will be labeled "crazy," be hospitalized, or be forced to live in some type of group setting.

Victims of violence (sexual assault, domestic violence, child abuse, or other violence) often require advocacy services. This requires not only skills in dealing with the victims and their relatives but also a knowledge of laws and legal procedures. Legal agencies such as police departments and district attorney offices also may have an authority in such cases that they do not have in other patient situations.

Emergency room caregivers or persons outside the health system who must be involved with victims of sexual assault may not be sensitive to the trauma suffered by the victim and may show a greater or lesser degree of insensitivity in examining, treating, or getting information from the patient. Such insensitivity may stem from a lack of experience, psychological problems relating to sexuality, or inability to handle the situation in any other way. The social worker, by interpreting to the care provider or staff of another agency what this experience has meant to the victim, may be able to bring about changes in the former's behavior so that his/her responses are appropriate to the circumstances.

Social workers often feel frustrated when they are working to develop appropriate care plans with patients because the system and its rules and regulations block their best efforts. A thorough knowledge of those rules and regulations along with the development of close relationships with agency personnel who have the power to make decisions will help to implement health care plans.

Agencies that provide direct services can be divided into two categories: those that are established organizations and those that are developed in response to emergency or temporary situations in the community.

Although established agencies may drop specific services or add new ones, for the most part their functions will be consistent with the mission of their agencies. Understanding the requirements for referrals and keeping abreast of program changes make it possible to work satisfactorily with such organizations.

Successfully using the programs of emergency or temporarily funded agencies can be more complex. Examples are emergency food and housing or employment programs that are funded for specific training purposes for a period of months. It is vital that social workers establish relationships that will ensure that they receive information not only at the time such new programs are formed but also when the programs are dismantled.

The specific patient population will influence which of those community resources are most frequently used. In some instances, home health care, socialization, and recreation programs may be most needed. In others, housing, employment or job training, and income maintenance programs may be in greatest demand. Clinical programs for senior citizens may rely on adult day care, transportation, wellness, and Meals on Wheels services. In any setting, the social worker should evaluate the patient, the family, and the availability of services. The patient should also receive counseling about the reasons for the referral and, when indicated, therapy should be provided to help the patient understand his/her negative reactions to suggested changes in his/her behavior or life-style. The referral agency needs to be informed of the patient's needs and expectations, and other descriptive information to assist that agency in working with the referral.

Because of the difficulty in working with some agencies, a social worker may choose not to approach agencies where appropriate services are available because the contacts on previous referrals have been unpleasant or unsatisfactory. A study done by the Department of Child Psychiatry, The London Hospital, showed that social workers made referrals to agencies from which help was available in a crisis, that offered opportunities to discuss the case, and with which there had been "previous positive contact" (Marks, Wolkind, & Napper, 1981). Whenever possible, it is important to resolve the issues of poor responsiveness rather than avoiding the offending agency. Documentation of specific problems taken to the agency's management staff may bring about a change in staff attitudes.

Most importantly, the social worker must be flexible in his/her efforts to achieve the goals of the health care plan. Agencies must be encouraged to act in the patient's best interest, whether it is done by coaxing or demanding that services be provided. At times it may be more effective to use established welfare rights groups and civil liberties groups in order for patients to be accepted for services.

INTERPROFESSIONAL COLLABORATION

It is not possible for the social worker to perform well as an advocate for the patient if the role and the skills required are not understood and respected by the other providers in the primary care setting. Physicians' perceptions of the skills and knowledge of social workers may not be accurate, and such misperceptions may lead to disagreements in the development and implementation of care plans for patients. Mizrahi and Abramson describe the "'disjunctures' evident in perceptions of patient care, attitudes toward knowledge and certainty in medicine and social work, perspectives on patients' rights, perspectives on teamwork, and the perception of social work by social workers and physicians" (Mizrahi & Abramson, 1985). Demonstrating professional skills and providing consistent feedback to colleagues verbally or in medical chart notes can dispel such misperceptions and reinforce the social worker's role.

Because of time and staffing pressures, most social work departments have found it useful to develop high-risk or priority criteria that other caregivers can use in making referrals. Case conferences, team meetings, and clinic rounds are additional means whereby the social worker may interpret the behavior or requirements of a particular patient and/or family and may also discuss available resources or gaps in services.

The establishment of multidisciplinary teams is effective in working with child and elderly abuse, Acquired Immune Deficiency Syndrome (AIDS) patients, and other diagnosis- or age-specific patients. Often the case manager role may be assigned to the social worker. Each profession brings its own point-of-view to the team, thus assuring a comprehensive care plan. Disadvantages of multidisciplinary teams may include differing approaches of the team members that may be discerned negatively by patients or family members. The expense of staff time spent in established multidisciplinary teams may deter their use. Experience with such teams, however, may show that the decrease in duplicating services and the provision of more focused care may actually cut down the time spent with and on behalf of the patient/family by all team members (Ludwig, 1981; O'Malley, Everitt, O'Malley, & Campion, 1983).

As social workers identify problems regarding the access to and the quality of the care provided within their own primary care settings, they may use internal advocacy to resolve the problems:

> Internal advocacy is an activity, engaged in by social work practitioners in their roles as professional employees, which is undertaken for the purpose of changing the formal policies, programs, or procedures of the agencies that employ them, in the interest of increasing the effectiveness of the services provided or reviewing organizational conditions or practices that are deleterious to the client populations served. (Patti, 1974)

Such internal advocacy may be handled by procedures established by the setting and may involve the administration of the social work department, the patient representative, or other medical or administrative staff. The social work department may call a meeting with representatives of other agencies who have expressed concern about the care given or the response to a particular patient. Recommendations should then be sent to appropriate personnel within the primary care setting. There are times in which the social worker deals directly with the physician providers to assure that the patient has received an appropriate level of care. For example, if a patient is being referred for placement by clinic staff, but the patient has not had a complete medical examination, the social worker should indicate the need for this before proceeding with the referral recommendations.

Although the social worker should function as a patient advocate within the primary care setting, this can create problems. If this role is formalized and the social work department or one of its staff members assumes the role of patient representative, grievances will be presented to the social work department for resolution, which can place the department in an adversarial role with the other health professionals. One way to avoid problems is to ensure that everyone in the setting is aware that the social work department is expected to act in this capacity. The administration of the setting is responsible for supporting the social work department in its recommendations.

ADVOCACY AND PROGRAM DEVELOPMENT

Although he was writing about advocacy as it relates to discharge planning, Lurie's identification of three areas of advocacy applies equally to primary care. These three areas are:

1. political advocacy — to improve governmental programs
2. resource development advocacy — to meet unmet needs
3. case advocacy — to ensure that programs are accessible to and appropriate for eligible patients and families. (Lurie, 1982)

Kulys and Moyer write that " . . . social workers need to continue to be instrumental in highlighting how the various societal stresses and injustices affect those who are poor and disadvantaged and help to clarify how lack of income and meaningful social supports affect health and the utilization of expensive health care services" (1985).

Three levels of intervention are needed to bring about change: 1) at the individual level, the person in control of the needed resource; 2) at the administrative level, the agency in control of the needed resource; 3) at the policy level, the political or social system which should be responsible for the resource which is lacking (Davidson & Rapp, 1976). When the level of responsibility has been identified, a plan may be implemented to obtain the needed resource, whether for an individual or a group of persons.

The use of a community advocacy group is vital in determining not only that needed services are provided but also that patients' rights are not abused. Examples are the various community groups which have developed in response to the needs of AIDS patients. The primary care social worker needs knowledge of the wide range of services provided by such organizations because of the positive effect such services may have on patients. Direct and supportive services are provided, but are no less significant than the legal interventions that can take place when a patient's rights have been denied or when there has been discrimination (Cecchi, 1986).

In writing about Adult Protective Services clients, Staudt notes the need to include "those services of a social worker who acts as an advocate and who may need to invoke legal action to enable the client's rights to be maintained" (Staudt, 1985, p. 205).

It can be frustrating for all members of the health care team when elderly persons who are legally competent refuse services that could enable them to live more comfortably and safely. This frustration usually stems from concern for the elderly person's well-being, but may be expressed by anger and/or rejection of the patient. The primary care social worker can help other caregivers to have a better understanding of the patient's need for independence (even though it may be self-destructive). Ongoing counseling with the patient on the part of the social worker may enable the patient to accept the recommended services.

Action taken by the social worker on behalf of a patient does not have to be limited to health care issues, but can or should involve an advocacy group or ombudsman with those incidents in which the patient has been treated unfairly and in which the social worker's expertise and action can provide changes in accessibility to services or programs.

Frequently, patients who live in nursing or alternative care homes receive ongoing care in a primary health care setting. At the time of their clinic visits, they may show evidence of malnourishment, poor physical care (decubiti, poor hygiene), maltreatment, or inattention to their medical conditions. Within the state or municipal governmental systems are departments and/or ombudsman programs established to investigate and deal with such conditions. The social worker must secure the consent of the patient or guardian and contact the appropriate authority with the complaint. Patients may be reluctant to have the matter pursued for fear of reprisals, but social workers should be aware of the safeguards inherent to such systems and inform the patient of them. Offering a follow-up visit to the facility in which the patient is living to determine that there has been no retaliation can be supportive to a patient. At times, a move to another facility may be necessary and the social worker should remain involved in the case until the situation is resolved. Whenever possible, the social worker should obtain feedback as to the outcome of the investigation, because such information will influence the use of the facility, and it can be shared with other members of the social work department.

Most professional organizations have advocacy and/or political action programs. Social workers can participate in such organizations or special interest groups and share the knowledge they have gained from direct contact with persons suffering from gaps in service, discrimination, or from underfunded governmental programs. Professional organizations are influential because of the numbers and backgrounds of their memberships.

A social worker from a primary care setting may be effective in serving on a panel questioning political candidates, to bring expertise about health care issues, including access and costs. Social workers, particularly those in public agencies, should be aware of the potential ramifications from such activities and should use annual leaves for participation in political activities during assigned working hours.

Experience shows that coalitions formed by professional organizations and community groups with similar goals frequently can be more effective than a single organization. The skills of social workers can be used to draw organizations together, help them establish mutual goals, and carry out activities focused on identified changes needed in services or systems.

A coalition formed by several organizations to advocate on behalf of homeless persons, for example, may take action on housing, employment opportunities, and children's access to school in addition to health care provision. Organizations have particular focus on the issue(s) for which they were established and can strengthen one another. Homelessness is only one of the critical societal problems for which alleviation of inadequate or nonexistent health care is only one action that needs to be taken.

Another form of advocacy is that of helping patients and/or families become involved in self-help groups. Rehr (1984) describes self-help groups as developing initially because of " . . . the failure of the social-health care system to meet the many on-going daily problems and needs of the chronically ill. . . . " Social workers may assist patients in joining established groups, or may develop a new group around a specific issue. Examples of groups are those for family members where an adolescent child has committed suicide, adult children who are caring for an aged parent, parents of twins, Alcoholics Anonymous, or caregivers for victims of Alzheimer's.

In writing about the self-help movement, Lurie states that it

> should be seen as complementary to professional treatment and to existing health programs. It is an extension of the preventative and rehabilitative processes which tap the resources of the client group and combine them with professional expertise. This movement demonstrates that clients and patients may have more resources than professionals have been able to develop and that these resources can be put to productive use. (Lurie & Shulman, 1983)

Activities the social worker may carry out include " . . . consulting, providing information and knowledge, linking groups to resources and services, training paraprofessionals in the organization and development of self-help groups, and in engaging in leadership training for group members" (Black & Drachman, 1985). Help may be given in finding a place for the meeting or in identifying possible speakers or consultants.

Program development is also a crucial activity for the social worker functioning in the advocacy role. Because services often do not exist when problems emerge such as AIDS, family violence, and homelessness, the social worker must be able to work with fellow professionals, colleagues, or coalitions to attempt to expand existing services or to develop new services. the primary care setting has status and data that can help justify the need to develop a new program for a particular population group at risk. Social workers can help physicians provide testimony at state and local legislatures, or can present such testimony themselves. This can be very effective, particularly when accompanied by supporting data. An example of such activity and use of data would be encouraging a state Medicaid plan to apply for a "heavy duty" Medicaid waiver that allows for greatly increased amounts of home health care and durable medical equipment. Social work departments can take the lead in collecting data and can involve other health agencies in sharing their data. Social workers often are acquainted with patients or their families who can provide a personal view in testifying before a legislative, governmental, or funding body.

An example of class advocacy concerns AIDS patients who often change in their eligibility for Medicaid depending upon their ability to work. Data documenting this fluctuation can be used with the appropriate state agency to support the broadening of Medicaid eligibility and other services not only for the patients of the clinic but for all AIDS patients in the state.

Social change can be a slow and tedious process. Physicians and health care institutions have power because they have status. They have power also because they usually have valid data to support the arguments that new programs are needed. The social worker needs to use that power effectively to create change more quickly so patients' needs can be met.

In summary, advocacy is an integral part of the role of the social worker in primary care because it can assure that essential services are provided for the patient to accomplish the health care plan. When services are not available, the social worker, in collaboration with others, should attempt to bring about the development of new programs to meet patient needs.

REFERENCES

Black, R. B., & Drachman, D. (1985, Spring). Hospital social workers and self-help groups. *Health and Social Work, 10*(2), 95-103.

Cecchi, R. L. (1986, August). Health care advocacy for AIDS patients. *QRB, 12*(8), 297-303.

Davidson, W. S., & Rapp, C. A. (1976, May). Child advocacy in the justice system. *Social Work, 21*(3), 225-232.

Encyclopedia of social work (18th ed., Vol. 1). (1987). Silver Spring, MD: National Association of Social Workers.

Kulys, R., & Moyer, R. (1985, Fall)). Good health, whose responsibility? *Social Work in Health Care, 11*(1), 63-84.

Ludwig, S. (1981, March). A multidisciplinary approach to child abuse. *Nursing Clinics of North America, 16*(1), 161-165.

Lurie, A. (1982, Winter). The social work advocacy role in discharge planning. *Social Work in Health Care, 8*(2), 75-85.

Lurie, A., & Shulman, L. (1983, Summer). The professional connection with self-help groups in health care settings. *Social Work in Health Care, 8*(4), 69-77.

Marks, F. M., Wolkind, S. N., & Napper, R. (1981, July-August). Primary care workers' perception of disturbed children and the agencies they use to help these children. *Child Care, Health and Development, 7*(4), 217-228.

Mizrahi, T., & Abramson, J. (1985, Spring). Sources of strain between physicians and social workers: Implications for social workers in health care settings. *Social Work in Health Care, 10*(3), 33-51.

O'Malley, T. A., Everitt, D. E., O'Malley, H. C., & Campion, E. W. (1983, June). Identifying and preventing family-mediated abuse and neglect of elderly persons. *Annals of Internal Medicine, 98*(6), 998-1005.

Patti, R. J. (1974). Limitations and prospects of internal advocacy. *Social Casework, 55*(9), 537.

Rehr, H. (1984). Health care and social work services: Present concerns and future directions. *Social Work in Health Care, 10*(1), 78-79.

Staudt, M. (1985). The social worker as an advocate in adult protective services. *Social Work, 30*(3), 205.

Chapter 6

THE CONSULTANT'S ROLE

Betty L. Rusnack

Physicians who seek to manage or treat the emotional, familial, and social problems of their patients can benefit from professional social work consultation. Social workers have had a long history of collaboration with other health care providers in professional education and in practice.

The literature on primary care identifies the need for social workers to participate with other members of the interdisciplinary team to accomplish comprehensive care objectives. It is known that 60% of all patient visits to physicians' offices are the result of psychosomatic, circumstantial, or functional problems. In a chapter titled "Directions in Social Work Training for Primary Care," Bess Dana points out that some physicians in primary care are not prepared to carry out such functions as:

> . . . the incorporation of the principles of prevention within the daily delivery of primary health care services, the establishment and maintenance of linkages with the inside world of the hospital and the outside world of home and community, the setting of priorities and selection of specific services in relation to the health needs of the population served, the preparation and support of the patient for the management of his or her own health . . . . (Dana, 1983, p. 156)

Guidance on the use of consultation as an essential social work role in the primary care setting is minimal, even though social workers for many years have been performing "educational" functions in clinical rotations of medical students and residents. Claudia Coulton, in *Social Work Quality Assurance Programs: A Comparative Analysis*, points out that little research has been conducted on the relative effectiveness of primary care providers who received professional consultation regarding the treatment of psychosocial problems (Coulton, 1983).

Barriers to social work's participation in primary care include the location of social workers outside of the mainstream of private practice of ambulatory medical care, the lack of third-party funding for social work in primary medical care, and the emphasis on technology rather than on psychosocial factors in the structure and process of service delivery. Implementation of the role of the social work consultant in primary care is hindered by both the lack of definition of such a role and the lack of preparation of social workers to carry it out.

This chapter attempts to define social work consultation in primary care through the following objectives:

1. To identify guidelines from social work's history and from other human services disciplines that are applicable to social work consultation in primary care.
2. To propose a "cognitive map" for charting the boundaries of primary care for use by social work consultants and medical consultees.
3. To list some of the interrelated premises that affect social work consultation.
4. To identify the various steps in the consultation process that clarify tasks within the four phases of work.
5. To provide examples that illustrate three forms of social work consultation.

GUIDELINES

Social work's history provides the following guidelines for social work consultation in primary care.

Guideline One: The social worker assists the physician in making a diagnosis that considers the biological, psychological, and social components of the person's situation. In the early 1900s Richard C. Cabot, M.D., in his work in the Children's Aid Society, experienced the assistance that social workers can provide to the physician in making a "complete" diagnosis.

> Later, when he saw some of the same children in his clinic, he realized how much better he was able to understand them and their diseases because he was familiar with their home backgrounds and other environmental factors. For a complete diagnosis, Cabot felt it was necessary to have information about the patient's home, diet, work, family, and problems. (*Encyclopedia of Social Work*, 1977, pp. 92-93)

During the several decades before 1940 when medical students' educations included training periods in outpatient departments of hospitals, social workers contributed information regarding the psychosocial aspects of patient care. The various components of educational and consultative roles were not operationally defined. Social workers were able to affect both the medical students and the physicians who were preceptors to those students. John D. Stoeckle, in a chapter titled "Curriculum Development and Training for Health Professionals: The Job Ahead," states that "In effect, the social worker was also the consultant to the medical doctor, long in advance of psychiatric liaison services of the 1950s, an interprofessional relationship that Cabot noted early" (1983, p. 138).

Guideline Two: Social work consultation goes beyond direct service to patients. Martin Bloom, in *Primary Prevention: The Possible Science*, views consultation as a means of more widely using the talents of the experienced person than if he were serving patients exclusively in direct services (Bloom, 1981). He points out how consultation has been viewed as a major technique and focus of community psychology, community psychiatry, and community mental health. The Community Mental Health Act of 1963 mandated consultation to further prevention activities as one of the services required of community mental health centers in which social workers play an integral part.

Guideline Three: The social work consultant incorporates social work values with a focus on social functioning. Mary Holmes Gilmore in her chapter, "Consultation as a Social Work Activity," states that the variations in social work consultation could be due to the training of the consultant being primarily an overlay of practice methodology and that no model for consultation has emerged. She states:

> . . . it is the responsibility of the consultant, as social worker, to promote the values and utilize the best knowledge of the profession regarding the

most favorable conditions and circumstances of social functioning. It is this kind of goal striving and value orientation which distinguishes the professional social worker from consultants who represent other disciplines. (Gilmore, 1963, p. 50)

Guideline Four: Social work consultation is advisory and relies heavily on a problem-solving process. A. Kadushin in his book, *Consultation in Social Work*, conceptualizes consultation in social work agencies and provides a definition that appears to be applicable to other settings:

> Social work consultation is a problem-solving process in which help, purely advisory in nature, is offered by the social work consultant to a consultee (individual, group, organization, community) faced with a job-related problem (having a social work component that requires the expertise of a social work education). (Kadushin, 1977, pp. 36-37)

Since the time of the seminal work of Helen Harris Perlman, *Social Casework: A Problem-Solving Process* (1957), social workers have used various frameworks for which problem-solving approaches provide an orderly social work process in work with individuals, families, groups, and organizations. Beulah Roberts Compton and Burt Galaway in their chapter, "Problem-solving: A Model for Practice," delineate problem-solving frameworks used by social workers:

> In general such models demand that the worker be successively involved with (1) recognition or definition of the problem and engagement with the client system, (2) goal setting, (3) data collection, (4) assessment of the situation and planning of action (5) intervention, or carrying out of action, (6) evaluation, and (7) termination. (Compton & Galaway, 1979, pp. 234-235)

Guideline Five: Social workers may provide case consultation, program consultation, or a combination of the two. A typology of the kinds of consultation that social workers provide is identified by Lawrence Shulman in "Consultation." He states:

> The two types of consultation most frequently described are case consultation, provided to other professionals, and program consultation, provided to agencies or other organizations. Case consultation usually involves a social work consultant working with line staff to assist them in providing direct services to patients. Program or organizational consult-

ation usually involves work with administrative staff and, in some instances, may focus on agency policies, programs, and procedures designed to enhance direct practice services.

An interesting third form of consultation is an important synthesis of the
two traditional forms. This approach uses the discussion of specific cases
as a starting point for the analysis of program and organizational issues.
(Shulman, 1987, p. 326)

Case consultation and program consultation may be adapted to the
primary care setting. In case consultation attention must be given to the
needs, wants, and situations of the patients for whom the physician has
assumed responsibility for providing care. The focus is on the provision
of care. This strengthens the decision-making abilities of the consumers of service to make informed health and medical usage choices
and the constructive coping capacities of patients regardless of their
physical, social, or psychological states.

In program consultation attention must be focused on the needs and
wants of the primary care medical provider in order to strengthen the
structure and process of care so as to promote the health and wellness
of the population being served. This must be accomplished also within
the limitations and potential of a cost-effective primary care service,
including the availability of human resources.

Synthesis of case consultation and program consultation may be
adapted to primary care also by starting with the specific patient
problems and moving to program development considerations.

Jonell Kirby (1985), an educator and guidance counselor who works
with health and human service systems, and Robert R. Blake and Jan
Srygley Mouton (1976), psychologists who apply problem-solving
methods to their work with business corporations, developed the following two guidelines that are transferable to social work with primary
care providers:

Guideline One: An approach to consultation based on humanistic
philosophy facilitates communication between consultant and consultee. Kirby states that consultation is replacing referrals for comprehensive treatment in health and human services. The cognitive, affective,
and reactive attributes of the consultant were detailed by Kirby in a
discussion of "the self of the practitioner." She states that the first order
of business in becoming a consultant is to become confident about
oneself and sensitive to one's perceptions (Kirby, 1985, p. 294).

Using humanistic philosophy as a base for the implementation of consultation, the consultant communicates warmth and friendliness to the consultee. "Identity" and "caring," which have the positive effect of bridging the gap between "me" and "you," are demonstrated, for instance, in questions that are open and noncontrolling of the consultee (Kirby, 1985).

Kirby lists such components of consultative practice and training as: accepting the feelings and uniqueness of self and others; thinking about the dynamics of the interaction between consultant and consultee(s) and among participants as relevant to the consultative process; making the consultee's reference point the focus for explanations, changes, and motivations (Kirby, 1985). These components are congruent with such social work practice concepts as self-awareness, nonjudgmental attitude, tuning in, starting where the patient is, enabling, facilitating, human ecology, and others.

Guideline Two: A "cognitive map" provides a sound base for navigation. By offering theories pertinent to the patient's situation, Blake and Mouton (1976) believe that the consultant helps the consultee to internalize systematic and empirically tested ways of understanding. Based on this formulation, an important consideration for social work consultation in primary health care is the use of theories and principles. They propose a theory spectrum ranging from trial and error, a nontheoretical basis for action, to theory expressed in the form of explicit hypotheses that can be tested, a theoretical basis for action. Within the spectrum they include "cognitive maps and conceptual systems" as an intervention which helps the consultant to chart a sound base for navigation and assists the consultee in following the course when the consultant is gone (Blake & Mouton, 1976). Lacking tested hypotheses, the formulation of a cognitive map or identification of conceptual systems could help social workers in their consultation with primary care medical providers.

COGNITIVE MAP

A cognitive map enables social work consultants to assess their knowledge of the unique characteristics of primary care services; to develop empathy with the consultee; and to determine the "threads" of the consultee's struggles in achieving an understanding of the psychosocial aspects of primary care services. This format can be a guide for

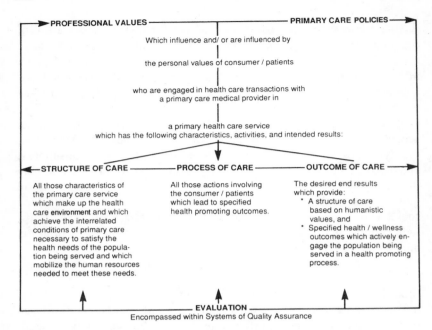

Figure 6.1 Paradigm: A "Cognitive Map" for Primary Care Consultation
Source: Adapted from Phaneuf, 1976, p. 20.

the social work consultant and the primary medical care consultee
when mutually assessing the "problems for work." It can also serve as
a useful reference for the consultee after consultation is completed.

Social work's value orientation provides the base of the guide. The
paradigm, however, is couched in frameworks familiar to medicine and
intended to facilitate open communication between health professionals who are from two different disciplines. Concepts are taken from
medical care administration, such as structure, process, and outcome of
care (Donabedian, 1966); from the application of health promotion and
prevention measures (Leavell & Clark, 1965); and from a life model of
practice based on human ecology (Germain & Gitterman, 1980). (See
Figure 6.1, Paradigm: A "Cognitive Map" for Primary Health Care
Consultation. Table 6.1, Glossary: Essential Interrelated Components
of a Cognitive Map for Social Work Consultation in Primary Health
Care, is found at the end of the chapter.)

The consultant provides service within the boundaries of primary
health care and the knowledge, value, and skill base of social work. The
goal is to assist the medical providers to understand better the needs

and wants of their patients and to assist them with problem solving. This role requires one to serve as a facilitator, enabler, and/or coach. As facilitator the social worker increases the ease of performance of the medical providers. As an enabler s/he strengthens the use of personal and community resources available to the primary care providers. As a coach s/he promotes the interpersonal skills of the providers in their transactions with individuals, families, groups, or communities.

INTERRELATED PREMISES

Consultation with primary care medical providers requires an understanding of social work values and knowledge; translation of primary care policies into goals and objectives; viewing primary care within the context of the organization and the practice of medical care in the United States; understanding fiscal matters influencing the organization and delivery of service; the systematic means for accomplishing the consultation process provided by the problem-solving approach; interventions that facilitate the work of the primary care physician; and a schema to help the consultee to internalize ways of working after the consultant is gone.

Following are 14 interrelated premises for the social work consultant to consider when working with primary medical care consultees:

1. The social work consultant must be clear about his/her identity as a person and as a health care professional who has expertise appropriate to primary care.
2. The social work consultant must understand the structure, process, and intended outcomes of primary care based on policies that promote accessible, comprehensive, continuous, coordinated care.
3. A "cognitive map" articulating the boundaries of primary care must be available to the consultant and the consultee to facilitate navigation through the consultative process.
4. While identifying with the objectives of primary care, the social work consultant must remain external to the system.
5. The transactions that take place between the social work consultant and the consultee must have the underpinning of social work professional values such as the worth and dignity of the person, self-determination, and interdependence.
6. Openness of communication must be facilitated by the consultant's skill in understanding the needs, wants, style, and orientation of the consultee.

7. A contractual working agreement must be established with the appropriate parties specifying allotted time, place, people, objectives, remuneration.

8. The focus of consultation must be based on the needs of the consultees and the patients they serve.

9. The consultee must be identified clearly, for example, primary care physician(s), primary care staff, primary care administrator, and so on.

10. If the focus of consultation is changed by the consultee or consultant, a new working contract must be agreed upon.

11. A problem-solving approach must provide the framework for the consultative process.

12. The consultant must advise the consultee with behaviors that facilitate, enable, and/or coach.

13. Fiscal considerations must provide a pragmatic screen to answer the question, "Will the options being considered work?"

14. Determination as to whether or not the stated contractual agreements are being met must be ascertained throughout and after the consultation process.

THE SOCIAL WORK CONSULTANT PROCESS

The social work consultant carries out activities by enabling the consultee to incorporate primary care goals and objectives into his/her practice; by facilitating mutual participation in a problem-solving process to effect changes that directly and indirectly address the needs of the population to be served; and through coaching activities to improve interpersonal skills with individuals, families, or groups. The work and the problem-solving steps are interrelated and concurrent.

Tasks of the social work consultant working with the primary medical care consultee are carried out in four phases: preaffiliation, beginning, middle, and ending.

Preaffiliation phase. The essential tasks of the preaffiliation phase are (1) marketing: becoming acquainted with the wants, needs, and resources of potential consumers, and (2) "tuning in": empathizing with primary care medical providers.

Marketing. A marketing process for attracting and holding prospective primary medical care providers who might want social work consultation is a task of the preaffiliation phase. This task requires the consultant to adapt business marketing processes and strategies to the problem-solving processes used by human service organizations. The goal of marketing to meet the needs of consumers is also a goal of social work. Gary Rosenberg and Andrew Weisman, in their chapter on "Marketing Social Services in Health Care Facilities," state that "Within the marketing definitional system, one of the major fits is that of consumer satisfaction, a main strategy in evaluative research on health care" (1984, p. 260).

The authors delineate a two-way marketing research process used to develop a marketing plan. Through the research process, factual information is gathered regarding consumers'/patients' preferences. This information is then sent back to the persons seeking consultation. A marketing perspective strengthens the primary care provider's ability to develop a service that the consumers/patients need and want rather than only those that the medical provider prefers to offer.

Essential to the Rosenberg and Weisman formulations is understanding of a "marketing audit." The purpose of the marketing audit is to formulate a longitudinal approach to assessing what the consultant has to offer that fits the primary care medical provider's needs. The audit has six components.

First, the consumer market and its segments are determined. What is the potential sphere of primary medical care providers for social work consultation and what are their needs?

Second, the organizational strengths and constraints of the social work consultant are scrutinized. Under what auspices is the social work consultant working, for example, self-employed private practitioner, hospital social work department, social work agency, public health agency, or other organizational entities? What are the strengths and constraints posed by these organizational auspices?

Third, the nature, extent, and significance of potential competition is ascertained. Who else, what other disciplines, are competing for the consultant role? What expertise do they have to offer that is different from or the same as that of social work? What do they charge?

Fourth, an inventory of the services offered to the primary care consultee are identified. What does the social work consultant have to offer? What qualifications or outstanding characteristics does the social worker have that pertain to primary care? The social worker determines, "Can I do the job?"

Fifth, the price of the consultation service is ascertained. What are the costs and the charges for the services to be rendered? If the consultant is working out of a sponsoring agency, what policy regulations regarding fiscal matters need to be considered?

Sixth, a plan for promotion of the consultation services is formulated. In what ways will the services of the consultant be made known to primary care medical providers?

Tuning in. The social work consultant already familiar with tuning in to the situations of patients can apply this skill to preaffiliation work with the primary medical care providers. Lawrence Shulman, in *The Skills of Helping Individuals and Groups*, lists four important factors that the social work consultant could apply and that raise questions to be answered in the preaffiliation phase:

1. Affective versus intellectual tuning in. The social work consultant tries to empathize with the primary medical care provider. What feelings does the physician have about social workers? What have his/her previous experiences been? Were they positive or negative? Were they personal or professional?

2. The social work consultant identifies his/her negative and positive feelings about the work to be done. How the consultant feels is how the consultant will act. What has the consultant experienced personally and professionally with medicine that will obstruct or enhance the work to be done? What are the consultant's feelings about some of the essential goals and objectives of primary care, for example, health promotion and disease prevention? For instance, is the consultant in touch with his/her feelings about such things as smoking, nutrition, living and working with chronic disease, or experiencing terminal illness?

3. Tuning in is done at a number of levels. The specific category of primary care within the context of medical practice in the community is considered. What are some opinions about primary care as a worthwhile or prestigious subspecialty in the community? What are the underlying feelings with regard to primary care of other doctors, health-related professionals, and patients? The unique characteristics of the specific primary care provider(s) with whom the consultation will take place are also important. Important considerations here include information about the background of the consultee, the nature of his/her practice, reasons for choosing primary care as a specialty, and education. The history of the consultee's medical practice individualizes him/her.

4. The specific phase of work in which the primary care provider is currently engaged provides a starting point for the work to be done. What educational or consultational background does the primary care medical provider have concerning the psychosocial aspects of medical care? How is the consultee currently carrying out primary care goals and objectives in his/her practice? What might be the new demands and need for change in the ways the consultee has to work if s/he is to consider new dimensions of practice? (Shulman, 1984)

Each aspect of tuning in must be considered as tentative and open to change. Consequently, tuning in is required throughout the several phases of the consultation.

Beginning phase. The essential task of this phase is to develop a "contract" or mutually acceptable working agreement. According to Lydia Rapoport in her article, "Consultation in Social Work," the major task of the beginning phase of work "is to establish a positive relationship and purposeful mode of working that develops through the consultee's repeated testing of the consultant's trustworthiness and usefulness" (1977, p. 195).

The cognitive map helps to identify problems or concerns. Previous work done by the consultant in marketing and tuning in provides a backdrop for paying attention to the particular concerns of the consultee. The social work consultant states the type of help available based on the primary medical care provider's statement of the problem, while maintaining the boundaries within which s/he has the knowledge, skills, and time to carry out the consultation process. The consultant and the consultee identify options regarding the work to be done. This determination of options indicates an openness by the consultant for deliberation within the boundaries of the consultant's expertise. Who is to be involved in the consultation process other than the primary care consultee, such as nurses, receptionists, managers, needs to be determined.

The working agreement should clarify when, where, and how the work will be done and who will do what. The contract is formalized by the consultant in a written statement that specifies goals, objectives, time schedule, activities with whom and where, evaluation schema, resources needed, and compensation. The agreement is reviewed by the consultee, and appropriate modifications are made.

Middle phase. The primary task of the middle phase is to carry out a problem-solving process. Here the consultant and the consultee state the problem, gather data, make an assessment, determine options, and choose a plan of action.

Statement of the problem. The beginning statement of the problems or concerns of primary care providers is likely to consist of areas that are irritating to them and that reflect their lack of know-how or success in achieving a solution. These problems may be related to direct work with consumers/patients, the program, or a combination of the two.

Such concerns may center on patients' noncompliance with medical orders regarding prescribed diets, taking medication as directed, and reducing or eliminating alcohol consumption. The concerns might be focused on the physician's lack of knowledge or experience with the health beliefs or habits of various racial, ethnic, or religious groups. The primary care provider may seek help in dealing with certain behavioral problems such as anxiety, depression, or hyperactivity; with understanding the psychosocial manifestations related to the person's stage in the life cycle; with gaining knowledge about community resources. Assistance might be sought in skill development in engaging the patient in the care process, in involving the family or peer group in the process of care, and in making and following through on referrals to social service agencies.

When the beginning statement of the problem centers on policies, procedures, or programs, the primary care providers may have concerns about providing a service that meets those needs of their patients that elude the provider. Some of the problem areas that might require consultation are: assisting in the development of a needs assessment; developing networks with long-term or terminal care facilities, special education programs, family service agencies, or community mental health services; and identifying such staff problems as morale, attitudes toward patients, or openness to implementation of primary care policies that may be impeding the work of the service. Although these areas are of concern, the social worker might best start the consultation with a presenting problem related to direct service with patients or to the organization.

Gathering data; making an assessment; determining options; choosing a plan of action. With the problem-for-work defined, the social work consultant and the consultee work together through the problem-solving process to gather data, make an assessment of the problems for work, and determine goals, barriers, objectives, and resources. Fiscal considerations are identified. What do the funding sources permit? What resources are available? A plan for intervention then needs to be chosen. The consultation may end when a plan of action has been determined, or it may continue through the implementation phase. The outcomes of all the interventions need to be evaluated and modifications instituted if required.

Ending phase. The essential tasks of the ending phase of the problem-solving process are evaluation and termination.

Looking back and looking ahead. The work of consultation is completed when the agreed upon objectives are reviewed by the consultant and the consultee. They determine what they have achieved together. Were the goals and objectives accomplished? What went right in the process? What were some of the difficulties? What would they do differently another time? A written summary of the work that was done and the results of the process provides an accounting of the actions taken. It also provides documentation that can be a useful reference in future work.

With the ending of this piece of work, the potential for future work together is raised. What might the primary care provider be interested in or need from the consultant in the future? What is the availability of the social worker if another situation calling for consultation arises? Does the social worker have the expertise needed or have in mind consultants who might be more appropriate?

THREE FORMS OF CONSULTATION

The following examples illustrate three forms of consultation: case consultation, program consultation, and synthesis of the two.

Case consultation. The presenting problem is how to respond to a 65-year-old widow who is considering suicide. In this example the social worker's expertise centered on her skill in knowing how to gather social systems information and how to make an assessment of the transactions involved (Spitzer & Welsh, 1981). The social worker and the physician listed the social systems pertinent to this woman's situation, and identified what was already known and what further information was needed. The woman had recently retired from a job in which she was employed for many years. She was dating a man who was pushing her to marry him. Her grown children were not in favor of the marriage. The physician was personally uncomfortable with the possibility of suicide. The social worker helped the physician to determine what, how, and when to explore further the woman's situation. Based on an analysis of the data gathered, options were listed and the patient and physician formulated a plan of action.

In this situation the social work consultant facilitated the assessment process, enabled the physician to gather more pertinent information from the patient, and coached the physician in carrying out a social systems analysis. The example illustrates how the consultant and consultee paid attention to primary care's emphasis on comprehensive care.

Program consultation. The objective of program consultation in the next example was to facilitate the continuing education of pediatricians regarding the biopsychosocial aspects of school-age children who were exhibiting hyperactive behavior. The problem was identified by a school social worker when elementary school special education personnel complained about the lack of informative medical data submitted by pediatricians in the community. The social worker's expertise centered on her ability to mobilize community resources. A needs assessment was carried out by the school social worker in collaboration with a Community Mental Health psychiatrist who was respected by pediatricians in the area. When the need for continuing education regarding hyperactive children was validated, the social worker assisted an ad hoc committee of pediatricians to design and implement a workshop. In this instance, the social worker reached out to pediatricians. She facilitated a needs assessment and the formation of an ad hoc committee. She enabled the committee to design and carry out a continuing education workshop. A primary care policy of coordination was put into action.

Synthesis of case consultation and program consultation. In this example the social worker started her work with the physician with the focus on his observation that the life situations of patients appeared to have a direct impact on their use of medical services. Based on the assessment of data, the agreed upon "problem-for-work" was for the physician to become more skilled in assisting patients to use their social support systems constructively. Using her networking skills, the social worker elicited options the physician could use in his direct service work with patients. A program issue that resulted from this beginning work was whether it would be possible to form self-help groups of patients to further the objective of networking.

The social worker's expertise in group formation and leadership was used to assist the physician in implementing such a program plan. The social worker facilitated the physician's goal of networking. She enabled him to form self-help groups and coached him regarding group development techniques. The promotion of primary care policies of comprehensive, coordinated, and continuous care guided the activities.

SUMMARY

Social workers have special knowledge and skill regarding the functioning of the person in the social environment that complement the primary care of the medical provider. The author hypothesizes that the social work consultant who is external to the primary care service system can serve as a facilitator, enabler, and coach to the primary care physician in order to strengthen the physician's skills in direct service to individuals, families, groups, or communities, as well as enhancing program design. Social workers must understand the market for their expertise and the fiscal constraints and potentials for providing primary care consultation. They must pay attention to the needs of providers and patients in ways that mobilize the human resources needed to meet these needs. This chapter set out to provide a framework for the social work consultant's roles and functions in primary care and to suggest tasks and problem-solving activities in the consultation process. Continuation of this work is needed in order to define more precisely social work consultant roles and functions in primary care, to implement the role as defined, and to measure effectiveness of the activities of the social work consultant in enhancing the achievement of primary health care objectives.

Table 6.1

Glossary: Essential Interrelated Components of a Cognitive Map for Social
Work Consultation in Primary Health Care

Care	The qualities of the transactions that show sensitivity to the needs and feelings of those who seek help. (Adapted from Sarason, 1985)
Consumer	One who freely chooses to purchase primary health care services or goods; seeks and uses information to determine the available options in the health care market and the potential use of the services or goods in meeting his/her needs; and who has the financial ability through third-party insurance or other means to purchase what s/he wants. (Adapted from Gummer, 1983)
Health	The ability of the person to carry out life tasks that correspond to age, interests, beliefs, and physical and mental capacities. Focus is on the promotion of strength and coping capacity regardless of one's physical or psychological state. (Adapted from Schlesinger, 1985)
Health Care Transactions	Reciprocal exchanges between consumer/patients and primary care providers leading to mutually agreed upon health care goals, objectives, and activities. (Adapted from Spiegel, 1971)
Patient	One who is a participant in a partnership with a primary care physician for the purpose of promoting health, diagnosing or treating disease, limiting disability, or attaining rehabilitation.
Personal Values	Those things that the population of concern hold in high regard based on demographic characteristics, needs, and wants.
Population of Concern	The panel of patients for whom the medical care physician has assumed responsibility for the provision of agreed upon health care services.
Primary Care Medical Providers	Family practitioners, internists, obstetricians, or pediatricians who provide longitudinal health care services to a panel of patients.
Primary Care Policies	Health promoting care that is accessible, comprehensive, coordinated, and continuous.
Process of Primary Care	Provision of first contact care. Assumption of longitudinal responsibility for care. Assumption of responsibility for supportive services. Provision of health and health-related services. (Adapted from Parker, 1977)
Professional Values	Human dignity; self-determination; interdependence.
Quality Assurance	Systems of evaluation and corrective action based on acceptability of care to consumer/patients and cost effectiveness and that conform to guidelines for professional standards of care as designated by voluntary and public agencies. (Adapted from Coulton, 1979)

REFERENCES

Blake, R. R., & Mouton, J. S. (1976). *Consultation*. Reading, MA: Addison-Wesley.

Bloom, M. (1981). *Primary prevention: The possible science*. Englewood Cliffs, NJ: Prentice-Hall.

Compton, B. R., & Galaway, B. (1979). Problem solving: A model for practice. In *Social Work Processes* (pp. 232-257). Homewood, IL: Dorsey Press.

Coulton, C. (1979). *Social work quality assurance programs: A comparative analysis*. Washington, DC: National Association of Social Workers.

Coulton, C. (1983). A social work perspective of research in primary care. In R. S. Miller (Ed.), *Primary health care: More than medicine* (pp. 210-228). Englewood Cliffs, NJ: Prentice-Hall.

Dana, B. (1983). Directions in social work training for primary care. In R. S. Miller (Ed.), *Primary health care: More than medicine*. Englewood Cliffs, NJ: Prentice-Hall.

Donabedian, A. (1966, Spring). Evaluating the quality of medical care. *The Milbank Memorial Fund Quarterly, 44*.

Encyclopedia of social work (17th ed., Vol. 1) Cabot, Richard Clarke (1865-1939). (1977). Washington, DC: National Association of Social Workers.

Germain, C. B., & Gitterman, A. (1980). *The life model of social work practice*. New York: Columbia University Press.

Gilmore, M. H. (1963). Consultation as a social work activity. In L. Rapoport (Ed.), *Consultation in social work practice* (pp. 33-50). New York: National Association of Social Workers.

Gummer, B. (1983). Consumerism and clients' rights. In A. Rosenblatt & D. Waldfogel (Eds.), *Handbook of clinical social work* (pp. 920-938). San Francisco: Jossey-Bass.

Kadushin, A. (1977). *Consultation in social work*. New York: Columbia University Press.

Kirby, J. (1985). *Consultation: Practice and practitioner*. Muncie, IN: Accelerated Development, Inc.

Leavell, H. R., & Clark, E. G. (1965). *Preventive medicine for the doctor in his community: An epidemiologic approach*. New York: McGraw-Hill.

Parker, A. (1977). Primary care—definition and purpose. In L. Corey, M. F. Epstein, & S. E. Saltman (Eds.), *Medicine in a changing society* (2nd ed.) (pp. 83-106). St. Louis: C.V. Mosby.

Perlman, H. H. (1957). *Social casework: A problem-solving process*. Chicago: University of Chicago Press.

Phaneuf, M. C. (1976). *The nursing audit: self-regulation in nursing practice* (2nd ed.). New York: Appleton-Century-Crofts.

Rapoport, L. (1977). Consultation in social work. In *Encyclopedia of social work* (17th ed., Vol. 1). Washington, DC: National Association of Social Workers.

Rosenberg, G., & Weisman, A. (1984). Marketing social services in health care facilities. In A. Lurie & G. Rosenberg (Eds.), *Social work administration in health care* (pp. 259-269). New York: Haworth.

Sarason, S. V. (1985). *Caring and compassion in clinical practice: Issues in the selection, training, and behavior of helping professionals*. San Francisco: Jossey-Bass.

Schlesinger, E. G. (1985). *Health care social work practice: Concepts and strategies*. St. Louis: Times Mirror/Mosby.

Shulman, L. (1984). *The skills of helping individuals and groups* (2nd ed.). Itasca, IL: F. E. Peacock.

Shulman, L. (1987). Consultation. In *Encyclopedia of social work* (18th ed., Vol. 1).
    (pp. 326-331). Silver Spring, MD: National Association of Social Workers.
Spiegel, J. (1971). *Transactions: The interplay between individual, family, and society.*
    New York: Science House.
Spitzer, K., & Welsh, B. (1981). *A problem-solving guide for effecting situational change.*
    Paper presented at Annual Program Meeting, Council of Social Work Education,
    Louisville, KY.
Stoeckle, J. D. (1983). Curriculum development and training for health professionals:
    The job ahead. In R. S. Miller (Ed.), *Primary health care: More than medicine*
    (pp. 135-152). Englewood Cliffs, NJ: Prentice-Hall.

Chapter 7

PUBLIC HEALTH ROLE

Matthew L. Henk

PUBLIC HEALTH SOCIAL WORK

Public health social work should not be defined by the setting in which one practices but how one practices in the setting. The public health role, unlike the generalist, therapist, or advocate roles, begins the intervention process by assessing the collective patient population rather than by assessing individual patients' needs. The primary care setting has some unique characteristics which allow a public health social work practice to develop and flourish. They include:

- a commitment to the concepts of health promotion and disease prevention;
- a willingness to assume the responsibility to provide comprehensive and continuous care. This requires multifocused interventions by a variety of health professionals to solve problems that adversely affect the health status of patients enrolled in the practice.
- data collection systems that will enable the social worker to develop health promotion/disease prevention programs for groups of patients who are at risk of becoming ill or having their illnesses continue with debilitating or fatal results.
- a radically different contract between provider and patient that allows the provider to intervene with the patient before the onset of illness and before services are initiated by the patient. Most other human service settings are categorical or specialized in nature, and provide services only after the problem has been identified and only after the patient has been diagnosed and referred by other agencies and individuals.

- physician providers that are trained to address both biomedical and psychosocial problems. These providers are more likely to have received training regarding the concept of the "interprofessional team."
- a specific and finite target population that can be identified and treated in a rational, organized fashion.

The public health role is significantly different from the other roles described in the text as it does not focus on a specific intervention for a specific patient at a specific stage of the disease process. Rather it requires many interventions, for both the patient and his environment, throughout the disease process continuum.

The setting and social workers should consider developing a public health practice because care can be provided more efficiently and effectively; the number of biomedical and psychosocial problems encountered in the primary care setting are so numerous that sufficient resources cannot be made available to meet all the acute care needs of the patients; and the disease process, if allowed to continue unchecked, will ultimately debilitate the patient.

This chapter will describe how a public health social work practice could be developed in a primary care setting using a five-phase problem-solving process:

- Assessment of needs
- Targeting interventions
- Prioritizing interventions
- Planning intervention strategies
- Evaluating the effectiveness of the interventions

Examples of the process will be provided later in the chapter.

ASSESSMENT

Assessment requires information or data. Chapter 8, "Record Keeping and Data Collection: Critical Elements for Quality Care" describes in detail the data collection systems available in most primary care settings. These systems include the registration file, the age/sex registry, and the diagnostic index (Froom, Culpepper, & Boisseau, 1977). These three systems provide the information needed to analyze and assess the patients enrolled in the practice. This analysis is the first step in the process of developing and prioritizing intervention programs for patients at risk.

Since specific and comprehensive data on patients is usually available in most primary care settings, high-risk patients can be easily identified to assess need. The questions: Who are the teenage diabetics? Who are the pregnant mothers who smoke, drink, or abuse drugs? Which young children reside in older homes with high concentrations of lead? are easily answered. With recent advances in computer technology, patients at risk can be identified in minutes. Case finding and outreach are not as much an issue in primary care setting as they are in other health care settings. Using city census data, a city health department might determine, for example, that 1000 children within a specified geographic area are at risk from lead poisoning. Because most city health departments do not usually have the names, addresses, and phone number of each of those patients, they may only be able to locate and screen 50 (or 5%) of those children that are at risk. In contrast, since primary care settings know the patients at risk and where they live, and have the necessary rapport with the patients, they should be more successful in their outreach and be able to screen 35% of those that are at risk (Henk & Froom, 1975). This percentage could increase if more intensive follow-up including home visits was provided.

INTERVENTIONS

Several authors have used matrices to identify targets of intervention for public health problems (Haddon, 1980; Margolis & Runyan, 1983). Such matrices allow the public health practitioner and the setting to view interventions in their totalities and not just in relationship to the acute phase of the biological problem. Knowing when and where interventions can occur for any given problem is essential in the development of a model matrix for public health interventions.

When. Because the disease moves along a continuum, it is important to know when a health promotion or disease prevention program should be developed. The "when" could be viewed in primary, secondary, and tertiary terms:

Primary Prevention includes activities undertaken to prevent the occurrence of disease. Examples include health education, encouraging the use of condoms to prevent AIDS, immunizations, and parent effectiveness classes.

Secondary Prevention includes activities undertaken to intervene after disease can be detected but before it is symptomatic. Examples are screening for lead levels, hypertension, cholesterol, and high-risk factors for child abuse, alcohol abuse, and AIDS.

Tertiary Prevention includes activities undertaken to prevent the progression of symptomatic disease. This includes the development and implementation of treatment programs for patients with common diagnoses, such as diet workshops for obese patients.

Where. The other component of the matrix identifies where the intervention will take place, that is, biological, individual/family, and environment. Biological includes molecule, cell, tissue, organ, or nervous system. Individual/family includes the patient, spouse, nuclear family, and extended family. Environment includes neighborhood, community, church, school, and government.

The matrix then could be viewed as in Figures 7.1 and 7.2 using AIDS and child abuse as the problems. This type of matrix not only allows the caregivers to view all the targets of intervention but also allows the various health professionals to clarify their roles in solving the specific problem.

After reviewing the various interventions identified in these matrices and projecting the same effort with other prevention efforts, one can see the enormity of the task. To meet the challenge it is essential that some of the interventions be transferred to categorical community resources who have accepted the responsibility to address specific health problems: that is, city, county, and state health departments, the Cancer Society, the March of Dimes, Alcoholics Anonymous, diet workshops, child guidance clinics, Community Mental Health Centers, Family Planning Programs, and so forth. In most cases these agencies are willing to satellite staff into the primary care setting or provide funds if sufficient need is documented and appropriate linkage agreements are developed that ensure both parties equally benefit from the arrangement. Some examples include:

> A community mental health center provides a part-time counselor to serve mental health patients at the primary care setting in exchange for receptionist time and space.
>
> A county health department provides funds to screen for lead poisoning or sickle-cell anemia. In exchange, the primary care setting would ensure that most high-risk children enrolled in the setting would be screened for lead levels and anemia and data be reported to the health department to further justify their program.
>
> The Cancer Society provides smoking cessation classes for patients of the primary care center as part of their ongoing effort to prevent cancer.

AIDS (HIV Prevention)

	Biological	Individual/Family	Environment
P R I M A R Y	Biomedical research to develop an immunization for AIDS.	Educating patient to the risk factors and prevention techniques. Ensuring the availability of condoms and clean syringes. Provision of psychosocial services to help the patient change risk-taking behavior.	Developing AIDS policies at the local, state, and federal levels. Developing better health education materials. Coalition building/legislative action to insure adequate funds and programs are available for research and education.
S E C O N D A R Y	Biomedical research to develop a better and more reliable test for AIDS.	Screening patient for AIDS. Providing information on how not to infect others. Screening population of the primary care setting to determine those most likely to be at risk, i.e., I.V. drug users, hepatitis patients, hemophiliacs; and to make screening tests available to them.	Identifying patients with high-risk behaviors and developing education programs for them in an effort to reduce transmission of the virus.
T E R T I A R Y	Biomedical research into potential cures for the virus. Research into methods to halt the progress of the disease.	Ensuring that AZT and other medications are available to patients. Educating the patients regarding immune system enhancement (reduce stress, proper diet, exercise, positive attitude, goal setting). Providing information regarding support groups, psychosocial service, legal assistance, and case management services.	Developing better treatment programs for infected patients. Group homes, hospices, specialty wards and hospitals. Providing continuing medical education for health professionals, including social workers. Ensuring confidentiality of patient's diagnosis. Legislative action to ensure that all patients are able to pay for treatment.

Figure 7.1 Some Targets for Intervening with Acquired Immune Deficiency Syndrome

SOURCE: Adapted from Haddon, 1980.

Child Abuse Prevention

	Biological	Individual/Family	Environment
P R I M A R Y	To ensure that adequate resources and social services are available to all parents and children. To ensure that appropriate, high-quality care is provided during pregnancy so child does not develop abnormal physical problems.	To ensure that childbirth education classes and parent effectiveness classes are available to all patients. To ensure that the other parent has an opportunity to attend the delivery.	To ensure that legislative action continues to provide adequate health and social service for families in need.
S E C O N D A R Y	To screen each child for signs of physical and sexual abuse.	To question parent(s) about discipline methods and their ability to cope with the stress involved in raising their children.	To ensure that legislation continues to require mandatory reporting of child abuse.
T E R T I A R Y	To ensure that each child receives high-quality health care, mental health care, and social services after the abuse occurs.	To ensure that families are provided with mental health care and social services to assist them to better cope with their situation.	To follow up regularly with the Department of Social Services to ensure that appropriate and adequate interventions are being provided by its staff. To assist in the development of child abuse task forces. To assist in the development of a multidisciplined team-approach to the problem. To advocate for children's rights.

Figure 7.2 Some Targets for Intervening with Child Abuse Prevention
SOURCE: Adapted from Haddon, 1980.

When such services are not available through local resources, it is essential that the public health social worker develop new programs to address these problems. This process begins by identifying patients with common problems. The educational and treatment programs will vary depending on the time and resources available to meet their needs.

The matrix on child abuse provides one example of how new programs should be developed. Parent effectiveness could be enhanced by providing individual counseling to parents, group sessions with guest speakers and videos, and home visits to new parents by county public health nurses.

In addition to these efforts it is essential that the power that is inherently associated with physicians and group practices be used to create change in legislation and institutional policies to better meet the needs of patients. The source of power relates primarily to the status of physicians or the group practice. In rural areas it also relates to economic power since a small primary care clinic is a significant employer and a required component of any viable small town. The number of patients also represents a significant power base when lobbying for various changes.

Social workers need to mobilize this power when they lobby for the linkages mentioned earlier. They also need to use this power base to ensure that legislation and policy positions do not adversely affect a specific population group.

To this end the social worker must be able to develop coalitions, consortia, committees, and associations to assist in this effort. Class advocacy of this type is also discussed in Chapter 5, "The Advocate's Role."

PRIORITIZATION

Presently, most decisions regarding the development of health promotion/disease prevention programs in primary care settings are subjective and arbitrary. To organize the process, the public health social worker must assist providers and administrators to agree on broad goals and specific interventions. The importance of this process cannot be overstated. Decision-makers in the setting ultimately want results and they need to define and set the goals for the social worker. This will help all parties avoid conflicting expectations. Because each setting will have different norms and values, the criteria for prioritizing interventions will vary. Interventions should:

1. Meet the goals and objectives established by the setting. If the setting receives public or private grant funds, interventions will need to meet local, state, federal or foundation funding requirements.

2. Address mortality, morbidity, age, and sex issues of the practice: What are the leading cause of death and the most commonly diagnosed problems of patients enrolled in the setting? What age group is most vulnerable?

3. Be inexpensive and realistic. The intervention should use existing categorical community services whenever possible to conserve the resources of the primary care setting. The social worker also needs to evaluate if the resources expended are worth the potential returns from the intervention.

4. Promote the setting's image and reputation as a comprehensive and prevention-oriented caregiver.

5. Improve the health status of a significant number of patients.

6. Be directed to those patients who are "most" or "least" likely to comply with the intervention plan. "Most" if you want to be effective; "Least" if you want to impact those who are most vulnerable.

For example, if one of the setting's goals is to improve the health status of the elderly and if a significant number of elderly were diagnosed as having had the flu during the previous year, then providing flu shots in conjunction with the city or state health department would be a high priority. Data in the age/sex registry would be available to identify the risk group, and existing staff should be available to develop and implement the outreach effort. Cost would be minimal, and the outreach effort would enhance the image of the clinic by demonstrating to the patients that disease prevention is more than idle rhetoric. The immunizations, known to be effective, would have a positive effect on the health of patients. It would also be cost-effective for HMO settings, as the time and cost to care for one patient who is hospitalized with complications from the flu could pay for the total outreach effort. Finally, the effort may also have the added benefit of increasing encounters and revenue for for-profit settings if patients have other health problems that require additional health services.

PLANNING INTERVENTION STRATEGIES

Once a problem is identified and an intervention is agreed upon, a care plan needs to be designed. Classic work planning process is needed to set objectives that are specific, time-phased, and measurable. Responsibility must also be assigned to individuals and agencies to carry out specific tasks (Public Health Service, Department of Health, Education, and Welfare, 1975; U.S. Department of Health and Human Services, 1980). The form from the U.S. Public Health Service Region VII work plan manual clarifies some of the elements of setting an objective for selected objectives regarding AIDS and child abuse (see Figures 7.3 and 7.4).

Each objective should relate to the broad goals agreed upon by the decision makers of the setting. Using the flu immunization outreach as an example, the objective might read, "To immunize 90% of all patients over 65 years of age." The milestones and action steps should identify each activity that must be accomplished to meet the objective. Individuals are assigned responsibility to accomplish each activity within a specific time frame. Milestones might include:

1. Obtaining the names and addresses of each patient over the age of 65.
2. Writing letters informing patients when and where they can be immunized.
3. Obtaining the inoculation from the city or state health department.
4. Assigning responsibilities to nursing staff to inoculate patients.
5. Mobilizing community resources to assist in patient transportation if necessary.
6. Setting up planning meetings to determine if immunization should be given during regular working hours, or on specific days during the week, or during evening hours.

Action steps further define tasks that must be accomplished if the milestone is to be met. Once again, a carefully laid out work plan will identify each step that needs to be taken to achieve the objective. Developing a written plan will also encourage the staff members to be accountable for their contributions in meeting the objective.

EVALUATION

If objectives are not met, the work planning process allows the social worker to determine where the process failed. New plans can then be developed for subsequent efforts to improve the health promotion/disease prevention program.

ORGANIZATION ENTITY ___Primary Health Care___

OBJECTIVE NUMBER ___1___

OBJECTIVE STATEMENT ___To provide childbirth education to 100% of all pregnant mothers to improve bonding in an effort to reduce child abuse.___

LAST DATE REVISED _____

OTHER ACTION	AGENCY ACTION	MILESTONE & ACTION STEP →	MILESTONE (Δ)/Action Steps (Δ)	Annual Target	1st Qtr.	2nd Qtr.	3rd Qtr.	4th Qtr.
	Public Health Social Worker	1	To arrange, with a local community resource, to provide childbirth education (CBE) class		X			
		2	To identify all pregnant participants		X			
		3	To ensure each patient is encouraged by their physician to attend. This can be accomplished during office visits, by phone or letter		X			
		4	To locate and secure space and time to hold the class		X			
		5	To ensure information is exchanged into the medical record when patients attend C.B.E. class		X	X	X	X
		6	Attend classes to identify problem areas		X	X	X	X

Figure 7.3 Annual Work Program

ORGANIZATION ENTITY __Primary Care Setting__

OBJECTIVE NUMBER __1__

OBJECTIVE STATEMENT __Provide AIDS Education to__

__100% of all patients enrolled as heads of__

__household__

LAST DATE REVISED _____

OTHER ACTION	AGENCY ACTION	MILESTONE & ACTION STEP →	MILESTONE (Δ)/Action Steps (Δ)	Annual Target	1st Qtr.	2nd Qtr.	3rd Qtr.	4th Qtr.
	Public Health Social Worker	1	Obtain health promotion brochure from the Centers for Disease Control		X			
		2	Develop cover letter		X			
		3	Obtain labels for all patients identified as head of household		X			
		4	Mobilize volunteers to stuff envelopes and attach labels and stamps		X			
		5	Arrange for film on AIDS from State AIDS Coordinator			X		
		6	Obtain meeting area to present film				X	
		7	Ensure physician and other appropriate representatives attend meeting				X	
		8	Present film					X

Figure 7.4 Annual Work Program

Evaluation can be viewed in terms of process and health status outcomes. Process outcomes are evaluated by measuring the success of each step required to meet the objective. Health status outcomes are evaluated by measuring the degree to which the patient's health improved. (See Chapter 8 for further information.)

The work planning process helps identify deficiencies in the system and the individuals or agencies that failed to meet their responsibilities. Well-developed plans should go further than evaluating process outcomes because the real objective is to improve the health status of the patients. Since the literature provides few examples of the successes and failures involved in the development of health promotion and disease prevention programs, it is important for public health social workers to collect information on all aspects of the intervention process and to publish their findings. With flu immunization as an example, the following questions could be answered.

1. Which patients participated (age, sex, marital status, income, etc.)?
2. What was the most effective means of inviting patients to participate (phone, letter, postcard, newsletter)?
3. What was the cost of the outreach effort?
4. What clinic hours were used most by patients?

Evaluation is commonly omitted from the problem-solving process, yet it is one of the most essential steps in developing successful outreach programs.

CONCLUSION

The public health role offers social workers a unique opportunity to solve individual family and society problems at various stages of the disease process. Most primary care settings need a health professional who has the skills to address health promotion/disease prevention activities. Social workers can meet this need if they can develop a structured and integrated approach to the problem-solving process. If interventions are to be successful, the public health social worker will need to provide a variety of direct services to individuals and families, mobilize community resources, develop new programs that will serve high-risk groups, advocate for social change, and utilize other health professionals and volunteers.

Significant positive changes will occur in the health status of enrolled patients if each step in the processes described in this chapter is followed. The setting will also benefit if it demonstrates to patients that it is concerned about the total health of the patient and is willing to provide more comprehensive services to accomplish this goal.

REFERENCES

Froom, J., Culpepper, L., & Boisseau, V. (1977). An integrated medical record and data system for primary care, III. The diagnostic index – manual and computer methods and applications. *Journal of Family Practice, 5,* 113-120.

Haddon, W. (1980). Advance of the epidemiology of injury as a basis for public policy. *Public Health Report, 95,* 411-421.

Henk, M., & Froom, J. (1975). Outreach by primary care physicians. *Journal of the American Medical Association, 233,* 256-259.

Margolis, L.H., & Runyan, C.W. (1983). Accidental policy: An analysis of the problem of unintended injuries of childhood. *American Journal of Orthopsychiatry, 53,* 629-643.

Public Health Service, Department of Health Education and Welfare. (1975, September). *Work plan manual.* Kansas City, MO: Public Health Service.

U.S. Department of Health and Human Services. (1980). *Program management: A guide for improving program decisions.* Atlanta, GA: Centers for Disease Control.

FURTHER READING

Carson, R. (1977, September). What are physicians for? *The Journal of the American Medical Association, 238,* 1029-1031.

Clinical data collection and retrieval systems for a small primary care setting. (1982). Rockville, MD: BCHS Publication accomplished under Contract No. 240-78-0056.

Draper, P. & Smith, H. (1975, October). The primary care practitioner – specialist or jack-of-all-trades. *The New England Journal of Medicine,* 903-907.

Eimerl, T.S., & Laidlow, A.J. (1969). *A handbook for research in general practice.* London: Livingstone.

Elliston, B. (1978, February). The social worker's role in family medicine. *Journal of Continuing Education.*

Farley, E. (1974). Implications of filing charts by area of residence. *Journal of Family Practice, 1*(3), 43-47.

Farley, E., Treat, D., & Baker, C. (1974). An integrated system for the recording and retrieval of medical data in a primary care setting. *Journal of Family Practice, 1*(44).

Froom, J. (1974). The age-sex register. *Journal of Family Practice, 9*(1).

Froom, J. (1974). Classification of diseases. *Journal of Family Practice, 1*(1), 47-48.

Froom, J. (1974). Diagnostic Index-E book. *Journal of Family Practice, 1*(2), 45-48.

Froom, J., Rozzi, C., & Metcalfe, D. (1973). Research comments: Computer analysis of morbidity reports in primary care. (Implications for a national morbidity survey). *Journal of Clinical Computers, 2,* 42-51.

Gilandas, A. (1972, November). The problem oriented medical record in a psychiatric hospital. *Hospital and Community Psychiatry, 23*, 336-339.

Goldberg, R. (1973, October). The social worker and the family physician. *Social Casework*, 489-495.

Guyman, J. (1978). Family practice in evolution. *New England Journal of Medicine, 298*(11), 593-601.

Haddon, W. (1968). The changing approaches to the epidemiology, prevention, and amelioration of trauma: The transition to approaches etiologically rather than descriptively based. *American Journal of Public Health, 58*, 1431-1438.

Hookey, P. (1978). Social work in primary health care. In N. F. Bracht (Ed.), *Social work in health care*. New York: Haworth.

Hove, B., Kruse, K., & Wilson, J. (1979). The social worker's role in family practice education. *Journal of Family Practice, 8*(3), 523-527.

Illich, I. (1974). Medical nemesis. *Lancet, 1*, 918-921.

Kaplan, D., & Plotz, C. (1974, February). A controlled analysis of medical students in a family practice program. *Journal of Medical Education, 49*, 154-157.

Lechnyr, R. (1984). Clinical social work psychotherapy and insurance coverage: Information on billing procedures. *Clinical Social Work Journal, 12*(1), 69-77.

Minnesota Systems Research, Inc. (1977). *Classification and codes for children and youth — social work*. Minneapolis: DHEW Training Grant #MCT-001036-02.

Olsen, K. M., & Olsen, M. E. (1967, July). Role expectations and perceptions for social workers in medical settings. *Social Work*, 70-78.

Rehr, H., & Berkman, B. (1973). Social service casefinding in the hospital — its influence on the utilization of social services. *American Journal of Public Health, 63*(10), 857-861.

Runyan, C. W. (1985). Health assessment and public policy within a public health framework. In P. Karoly (Ed.), *Measurement strategies in health psychology* (pp. 601-627). New York: John Wiley.

Shulman, L. E., & Mantell, J. E. (1988). The AIDS crisis: A United States health care perspective. *International Journal of Social Sciences and Medicine, 26*(10), 979-988.

Treat, D., & Henk, M. (1978). Utilization of community resources. In R. Rakel (Ed.), *Family practice*. Philadelphia: Saunders.

Tunner, L., & Carmichael, L. (1970, November). The role of the social worker in family medicine training. *Journal of Medical Education, 45*, 859-865.

U.S. Department of Health & Human Services. (1980). *How to speak primary care*. Rockville, MD: Public Health Service.

Whitby, L. (1974, October). Screening for disease. *The Lancet*, 819-821.

Chapter 8

RECORD KEEPING AND DATA COLLECTION
Critical Elements for Quality Care

Matthew L. Henk

The health care industry has developed some new and unique record keeping and data collection systems during the past 15 years. The systems were designed to assist with patient care, to bill and collect for services, to manage the business in an efficient manner, to evaluate the quality of services, to avoid medical legal problems, and to perform a variety of other functions. The social worker must have a complete understanding of the medical record and the manual and computerized data collection systems if the goals of service delivery, quality assurance, accountability, and research are to be achieved.

The following chapter provides a review of the problem-oriented method of record keeping, describes the various data collection and tracking systems, and demonstrates how these systems could improve health care delivery.

PROBLEM-ORIENTED MEDICAL RECORD (POMR)

Social workers employed in a progressive primary care setting should have few problems entering into the medical record information regarding patient problems. Entries in the progress notes of the medical

NOTE: This chapter was prepared by a government employee as part of his official duties; therefore, the material is in the public domain and may be reproduced or copied without permission.

record will have to conform to the system that exists in the host setting. Most settings will be using the problem-oriented medical record (POMR) system described by Dr. Lawrence Weed in his text *Medical Records, Medical Education, and Patient Care*, (1969) and by Drs. John Bjorn and Harold Cross in their text *The Problem-Oriented Private Practice of Medicine* (1970). This system has been instituted in most primary care settings to improve communications and diagnostic judgment. Integrating social work information into the medical record system provides the following advantages:

1. Continuity and effectiveness of patient care is contingent upon the medical record serving as the primary system of record keeping and communication within the primary care setting.
2. Information that social workers provide is essential to the physicians and other health care professionals who need to be aware of the patient's emotional, familial, and socioeconomic condition.
3. Quality of care can be measured by systematic chart review.
4. Data can be organized and collected, which will allow social workers to develop programs for high-risk patients.
5. Tracking systems can be implemented to ensure that referrals and health care plans are accomplished.
6. Medical legal problems can be minimized.
7. Health status and process outcomes can be measured for research and accountability purposes.

The POMR system allows for specific problem identification and concise record keeping through which patients' problems can be examined in a logical and sequential way that is readily retrievable by all staff. Dr. Weed suggests four phases of action:

1. The collection of data, medical history, physical examination, and laboratory data.
2. Formulation of problems.
3. The development of a plan and treatment of each problem.
4. The follow-up through the use of numbered entitled progress notes for each problem. (Weed, 1969)

Essential to the implementation of POMR is the listing of all significant patient problems on a cumulative or master problem list. (See Figure 8.1.) In practice the list is kept conspicuously in the medical record, usually on the first sheet to the left side of the record. The primary advantage of having a master problem list is that it allows the person reviewing a chart to determine quickly the major medical, socioeconomic, and emotional problems that are facing the patient, without reviewing each note in the record. The decision to list a problem on the cumulative problem list is subjective but is based essentially on its future usefulness in being identified as a significant problem.

The other essential component of the POMR is the standardization of recording information regarding a specific problem. Briefly, one must record:

1. The problem or diagnosis.
2. The subjective data or information provided by the patient regarding his/her problem.
3. Objective data or information regarding the patient that is documentable in terms of more empirical findings: that is, lab and other tests.
4. The analysis of the subjective and objective data.
5. The plan that includes treatment, further diagnostic workup, and patient education.

This is commonly known as the SOAP (Subjective Objective Analysis Plan) format. This system allows the provider and others to understand how the previous person diagnosed the problem and reinforces systematic thought regarding problem identification and treatment.

In order for the information recorded in the chart to be organized and collected systematically, each problem should be coded. Presently, most primary care settings use the International Classification of Diseases 9th Revision Clinical Modifications (ICD-9-CM) (1980). The coded data can then be collected manually or through a computer. The ICD-9-CM is usually accessible in most settings and can be expanded to accommodate additional problems. Some of the psychosocial codes found under the "V" classifications of the ICD-9-CM include:

Mental and Behavioral Problems
Problems With Learning
Problems With Communication
Other Mental Problems
Other Behavioral Problems
Unspecified Mental or Behavioral Problems
Other Family Circumstances
Family Disruptions
Parent Child Problems
Child Abuse

Problems With Aged Parents or In-Laws
Health Problems Within the Family
Unemployment
Social Maladjustment

The ICD-9-CM classification system covers a variety of psychosocial problems, but it does not have specific criteria to define the parameters of each problem nor does it provide for an adequate number of problems.

The lack of standard terminology for psychosocial problems is a major concern when social workers have to record their progress notes. Until a mutually approved and professionally endorsed social work classification system is developed, social workers will have to continue to use those psychosocial codes available through the ICD-9-CM or the *Diagnostic and Statistical Manual of Mental Disorders, III Revision* (DSM III) (1980). The National Association of Social Workers is attempting to solve this problem through a new coding system that is in the developmental stage.

In addition to the completion of the progress notes, an encounter form should be filled out for each office visit. (See Figure 8.2.) This form will be used to bill the patient (if the setting charges for social work service) and to record information about the type of problems that are being seen.

DATA COLLECTION AND TRACKING SYSTEMS

Information collected from the encounter form, patient registration, and other manual and computerized data collection resources can be used to identify patients by age, sex, diagnosis, and geographic residence. This data allows the social worker to identify patients who have common problems or risk factors. The following are the most useful manual data collection systems now available.

Patient registration file. The patient registration file is designed to collect basic information on a health center's patient population and is the master index to the medical records file. (See Figure 8.3A.) Cards are filed alphabetically by the patient's last name. The minimum data set that should be collected includes: patient's name, date of birth, sex, and medical record number. The patient registration card also includes the patient's address, telephone number, source of payment, primary provider, date of registration, date of inactivity, and emergency contact. Because the major purpose of the patient registration file is to serve as a reference tool for use during a specific patient encounter or visit to the health center, each card must be filed by the patient's last name for easy access. This method of filing severely limits its usefulness in easily identifying patient age/sex groups for both internal and external reporting purposes. The Age/Sex Registry and Diagnostic Index have been designed to fulfill this function.

The age/sex registry. The age/sex registry consists of a collection of 3 × 5 cards, one for each patient. The cards, color-coded blue for males and pink for females, contain the following information: name, date of birth, marital status, census tract or chart number identification of physician by code number, date of entry into the practice, and date of removal from the practice. Cards are filed by year of birth; males are grouped separately from females, and cards are arranged alphabetically within each section. Cards are maintained for "active patients" only. One definition of an "active patient" is one who belongs to a family from which one member visited the practice in the preceding two years. (See Figure 8.3B.)

The diagnostic index-E-book. The diagnostic index-E-book is a looseleaf binder containing 3 × 5-inch sheets of paper filed in an over-lapping or "shingled" manner. There are one or more sheets for each diagnostic rubric or code number. The ICD-9-CM can be used to classify health problems for this system. The E-book sheets contain the following information: date of encounter, patient's name, type of epi-sode (diagnoses newly made are recorded as "N" [new]; those that have been made by a previous physician and are still existent are recorded as "O" [old]), date of birth, a disposition code, and physician's or other health provider's name. If multiple diagnoses are made, the same information is recorded on the appropriate sheets for each diagnosis. Diagnoses of chronic conditions such as diabetes mellitus or hyperten-sion are recorded only once for each patient. Acute self-limited prob-lems such as otitis media or pharyngitis are recorded each time they occur (Henk & Froom, 1975). (See Figure 8.4.)

Census tract or geographic filing systems. Patients' charts can be filed alphabetically within census tracts or other geographic boundaries in which these patients reside. Census maps and census tract directories listing all addresses within a given census tract are available from the Federal Bureau of Census. However, if the primary care centers do not file this way, geographic residence can also be found in patient registra-tion files.

Referral log. The referral log is designed to monitor the type and frequency of referrals (usually to outside agencies) and to assure that a report is received for each referral. The log entry is initiated at the time the referral is made and is completed when a report is received. The referral log also includes the reason for the referral and the date of the referral appointment.

The log can be used in conjunction with a pending referral file in which a copy of the referral form is filed alphabetically by month of referral. When the report is received, the copy is pulled, the receipt date noted, and the log completed. (See Figure 8.5.)

Tickler file. The tickler file is designed to identify patients who should be monitored for care and follow-up. Health center providers must select the criteria for this file, such as patients with chronic diseases and women with high-risk pregnancies. If there is a long period between appointments for care, such as for immunization shots, the tickler file is particularly helpful to center staff in reminding patients of needed care. A health center can use the file to generate reminder cards for future appointments and/or to follow up on patients who missed their appointments. A card is created for each patient who is to be followed and is filed alphabetically by month of next visit. In addition, the patient's chart should indicate that there is a tickler card, so that the card is pulled when the chart is pulled. The minimum data set includes: patient name, birthdate, sex, medical record number, date of next appointment, and an indicator of whether or not the appointment was kept. The tickler card also includes provider name, reason for tracking, type of service, address, phone number, and dates that reminders were sent/telephone calls were made (U.S. Department of Health and Human Services, Bureau of Health Care Delivery and Assistance, 1982). (See Figure 8.6.)

Smaller settings may have such manual systems, but if they do not, the social worker could play a pivotal role in the development and implementation of these systems. In larger settings computers will probably store this information automatically, provided the software is designed properly. Unfortunately, retrieval of data from the computer regarding the patient's age, sex, diagnosis, and area of residence is usually difficult because most software systems have been developed to accommodate practice management goals rather than patient care goals. If the social worker can demonstrate the value of accessing this information, the software could be changed to accommodate patient care, quality assurance, research, and accountability goals.

PATIENT CARE GOALS

Data can have a significant positive effect on patient care when they are used to develop programs for high-risk patients and to track compliance with health care plans.

Because health promotion and disease prevention programs for high-risk patients are discussed at length in an earlier chapter, "Public Health Role," the following is provided as only a brief explanation of this concept. Patient information regarding age, sex, diagnosis, geographic area, or combinations thereof can be retrieved to identify at-risk population groups. Once these high-risk groups are identified, primary, secondary, and tertiary prevention interventions can be developed to reduce their risks. These programs might include providing flu shots for patients who are over 65 years of age and those who have significant heart and lung problems; providing parent effectiveness classes for patients with the diagnosis of "parent child conflict," "failure to thrive," or "child abuse"; providing weight reduction services for obese, hypertensive, or diabetic patients.

Another significant goal for all health care providers is to achieve patient compliance with the health care plan. If adequate tracking systems are in place, the potentially noncompliant patient can be identified. Once identified, follow-up procedures can be developed to assure health care plans are achieved. Although the patient is ultimately responsible for compliance, the primary care center should provide appropriate referrals and mobilize all available resources needed to achieve compliance. The tickler file and referral log, described earlier, were designed to accomplish this goal.

QUALITY ASSURANCE GOALS

Many elements of quality assurance such as the training and experience of staff do not relate directly to data. Data are essential, however, to the development of a needs/demand assessment and a social service plan, both of which are key ingredients for any quality assurance program. Data from that plan should include the number and nature of the problems seen by the social work department as a whole and by individual staff.

PROCESS OUTCOMES/PEER REVIEW

Another element of quality assurance is the implementation of a peer review system using retrospective chart audits according to diagnosis. This requires monthly review of charts according to a specific problem or diagnosis. Each problem should have specific criteria for the diagnosis, and treatment protocols to refer to when the audit team reviews the chart. For example, suspected child abuse should be evidenced by bruises, fractures, or some other objective findings, and referral to an appropriate child abuse program should be a requirement of any plan because it is required by law in most states.

Auditing charts can determine if records are complete, if data support the diagnosis, and if plans were appropriate to the problem. Monthly audit reports can be used to provide administration with some degree of assurance that quality services are being provided by the social work department.

HEALTH STATUS OUTCOMES MEASURES

If the problem-solving process is followed correctly, the patient could have some positive change in his/her health status. Changes in health status are difficult to measure, and it is even more difficult to relate these changes directly to the social worker's intervention. If a problem is identified as "truancy," for example, and the criterion is that the patient has more than five days of unexcused absence from school a month, then an improvement in health status will be accomplished when a reduction in the length of unexcused absence occurs. Attributing change directly to the implementation of a specific plan by the social worker is difficult because there are many other variables involved.

If data are consistent among social work departments in various primary care settings, however, it is possible to measure the efficacy of different treatments for specific problems based on shared data. When we as social workers can document that, or when interventions positively influence health status, then payment for social services becomes a real possibility.

RESEARCH GOALS

The relationship between organic health problems and behavior is not always clearly documented because data regarding the patient's psychosocial problems might not be recorded in the health center's data collection systems. This relationship is crucial to understanding illness and wellness. If psychosocial data were available, a variety of research questions centering on patient profiles and effective treatment could be answered. Such questions might include:

1. What is the psychosocial profile of the compliant or noncompliant teen-age diabetic?
2. Can obese patients lose more weight if they are in competition with others who also want to lose weight?
3. Do patients with pediatric respiratory disorders live in areas that have high levels of air pollution?
4. What is the health status of parents of abused children? Do these parents have a high incidence of chronic disease or have a major physical or mental health problem?
5. What agency or therapist is most effective in treating the depressed or anxious patient?
6. Are problems of truancy or drug dependency related to specific school districts?

Research involving psychosocial problems often lacks validity because there are insufficient numbers to substantiate research findings. This problem could be alleviated if psychosocial problems were standardized, thus enabling social work departments from several primary care settings to collaborate on research projects through pooled data. The primary care setting will stimulate many research ideas; and unlike other health care settings, the primary care setting usually has the data available to accomplish research goals.

ACCOUNTABILITY GOALS

Several hospital social work departments are developing systems that will collect data on the patient, the patient's problems, the type of service provided, and the time involved in providing the service. To some degree each social work department has a tool to document its activities. Although these systems are needed and provide good data, they often lack credibility because they are not linked directly to the data system of the health center: that is, the patient registration file, the medical chart, the encounter form, and others. Standard reports using data from these systems should be submitted to administration monthly to document the quantity and quality of services being provided.

CONCLUSION

Understanding how to collect and use data is critical if social workers intend to become an integral part of the primary care movement. The process begins with the medical record and a complete SOAP-formatted progress note. A mutually approved and professionally endorsed system to classify psychosocial problems is also essential to this process.

The collection of data by medical diagnosis, age, sex, and geographic area will allow social workers to develop programs for at-risk population groups, accomplish research, evaluate quality of care, and document that the social work department is accomplishing its goals and objectives.

PROBLEM LIST

Problem Number	Code No.	Problem	Date Noted	Date Resolved
1	134	Depression	3/1/88	8/1/88

Figure 8.1 Problem List

DATE	NAME			DOCTOR OF VISIT		CODE	PRIMARY DOCTOR	
FAMILY NO.	ADDRESS					CENSUS TRACT		TEAM
BILL TO NO.	HEAD OF HOUSEHOLD			DATE OF BIRTH	B CODE	APPT TIME	ARRIVAL TIME	ROOM
INSURANCE 1		INSURANCE 2		INSURANCE 3			DISABLED FROM	
CONFIRMED	WORKER'S COMPENSATION	INSURANCE 4		INSURANCE 5			DISABLED TO	
BILL TO PATIENT	MOTOR VEHICLE ACCIDENT	COMMENTS/ALSO TO SEE					MAY RETURN TO WORK	
BILL TO INSURANCE	DATE OF INJURY							

CODE	SERVICES	CHARGES	CODE	LAB	CHARGES	CODE	PROCEDURES	CHARGES
0011	BRIEF RECHECK		8411	CBC, RBC, WBC HCT, HGB, DIFF		651-	AUDIOMETRY	
0012	ROUTINE		8413	RBC ONLY		641-	VISION	
0013	COMPLEX OR NEW PATIENT		8414	WBC ONLY		6211	EKG	
0014	PREMARITAL 1 2		8415	HCT ONLY		6212	RHYTHM STRIP	
0015	LAB		8416	HGB ONLY		3901	EAR IRRIGATION	
0016	DIAPHRAGM/IUD RECHECK		8417	DIFF. ONLY		631-	PROCTOSCOPY	
0017	PROCEDURE ONLY		8418	INDICES		632-	SIGMOIDOSCOPY	
0021	INITIAL PE - PART I		844-	SED RATE		644-	TONOMETRY	
0022	INITIAL PE-PART II		8422	RETIC COUNT		661-	VITALOR	
0023	INITIAL PE - COMPLETE		885-	EOS SMEAR		397-	EAR PIERCING	
0024	ANNUAL ADULT PE		8513	MONOSPOT		394-	DIAPHRAGM FITTING	
0025	ROUTINE FORM PE		8421	SICKLE DEX		392-	IUD INSERTION	
0026	PE 5-16 YRS.		8267	GTT ADMINISTRATION			TYPE ▶	
0027	PE <5		8519	COLD AGGLUT. (SCREEN ONLY)		891-	PAP	OUTSIDE CHARGE
0031	COUNSELING-MIN <30 >30		835-	VDRL/ART		OTHER (SPECIFY):		
0032	CONSULTANT - INITIAL		8281	LEAD SCREEN				
0033	CONSULTANT - FOLLOWUP		872-3	U/A MICRO ☐			INJECTIONS	
0041	OB INITIAL		873-	URINE COLONY COUNT		271-	DPT	
0042	OB RECHECK		872-	SENSITIVITIES IF +		272-	DT	
0043	POST PARTUM		814-	PREG TEST (URINE)		261-	OPV	
0045	PRE/POST SURGERY		804-	HOME GUAIAC		273-	MMR	
0051	HOME		871-	THROAT CULTURE		8351	TINE	
0052	AFTER HOURS		870-	OTHER CULTURE (SPECIFY):		8552	PPD	
0061	NURSE			WET MOUNT		267-	INFLUENZA	
0062	ALLERGY			KOH PREP		266-	PNEUMOVAX	
0063	SUTURE REMOVAL			GRAM STAIN		OTHER (SPECIFY):		
0064	3 BP VISITS 1 2 3			SEMEN ANALYSIS (P.V.)				
0065	THROAT PROTOCOL			SEMEN AN. (FERT. STUDY)			X-RAY	
0067	NURSE HOME S C					CHEST	OTHER (SPECIFY):	
OTHER (SPECIFY):				OUTSIDE LAB				
SURGERY (LACER/FRACT):			SPECIFY:			INDICATIONS:		
LOCATION:							SUPPLIES	
METHOD:						SPECIFY:		
LENGTH:			800-	LAB SERVICE CHARGE				
PROCEDURE CODE:			PATIENT WAITING ☐					
			NO SCREENING ☐					

PAYMENT EXPECTED AT TIME OF VISIT
ALL CREDITS APPLY TO OLDEST BALANCE.
THIS IS THE ONLY STATEMENT YOU WILL
RECEIVE WITHOUT AN ADDITIONAL CHARGE.

	CASH (AMOUNT)	CHECK (AMOUNT)	CASH DISCOUNT (AMOUNT)	TOTAL CHARGE ▶
DISPOSITION	NEXT APPOINTMENT	WITH F.M. PROVIDER	REASON	AMOUNT OF TIME NEEDED 15 30 45 60 MIN.	NOT TO SEE NP ☐

WRITTEN DIAGNOSIS FOR INSURANCE	
ADDITIONAL INSTRUCTIONS	
PATIENT EDUCATION	

X SIGNATURE

Figure 8.2 Patient Encounter Form

Side 1

```
+-----------------------------------------------------------+
|                   PATIENT REGISTER                        |
|                                                           |
| Name_____DOB_____Sex____#_____|
|                                                           |
| Address_____       |
|                                                           |
|          _____       |
|                                                           |
| Phone_____/_____       |
|              (Home)              (Work)                   |
| Payment Source(s)_____#_____        |
|                                                           |
|                  _____#_____         |
|                                                           |
| Primary Provider (Team)_____        |
|                                                           |
| Date Registered_____Date Inactive_____     |
+-----------------------------------------------------------+
```

Side 2

```
+-----------------------------------------------------------+
| Emergency Contact:                                        |
|                                                           |
| Name_____Phone_____/_____  |
|                                          (Home)  (Work)   |
| Address_____        |
|                                                           |
|          _____        |
|                                                           |
|          _____        |
|                                                           |
| Relationship to Patient_____        |
|                                                           |
|                                                           |
+-----------------------------------------------------------+
```

Figure 8.3A Patient Registration Card

```
┌─────────────────────────────────────────────────────────────────┐
│                    AGE/SEX REGISTRY CARD                          │
│ Name_____DOB_____ Sex_____#_____      │
│ Primary Provider (Team)_____     │
│ Date Registered_____     │
│ Chart #_____                                              │
│                                                                   │
│                                                                   │
└─────────────────────────────────────────────────────────────────┘
```

Figure 8.3B Age/Sex Registry Card

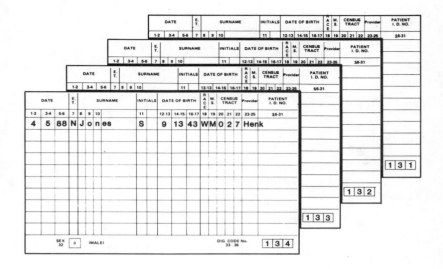

1. Columns 1–6: Code the date the problem was identified.

2. Column 7: Codes if the case was (N) new or (O) old.

3. Columns 8–10: Code the first three letters of the last name with space for completion.

4. Column 11: Code the initial of the first name with space for completion.

5. Columns 12–17: Code the date of birth.

6. Column 18: Race

7. Column 19: Marital status

8. Columns 20–22: Census tract or chart number

9. Columns 23–25: Provider

10. Columns 26–31: patient I.D. no.

Figure 8.4 E-Book Example

REFERRAL LOG

Week/Month and Year: _____   Page ____ of ____

Date	Medical Record #	Patient Name	Referring Provider	Referral MD/Specialty	Reason for Referral	Appt. Date	Date Report Rec'd.

Figure 8.5 Referral Log

Side 1

TICKLER CARD					
Name_____DOB _____Sex____ #_____					
Provider_____Reason:_____					
Type of Service	Due	Done	Type of Service	Due	Done

Side 2

Address:	Reminder Sent or Telephone Call Made:
_____	_____
_____	_____
_____	_____
Phone Nos.:	_____
_____ (Home)	
_____ (Work)	

Figure 8.6 Tickler Card

REFERENCES

Bjorn, J. C., & Cross, H. D. (1970). *The problem-oriented private practice of medicine.* New York: McGraw-Hill.

Diagnostic and statistical manual of mental disorders (3rd ed.). (1980). Washington, DC: American Psychiatric Association.

Henk, M., & Froom, J. (July 21, 1975). Outreach by primary care physicians. *Journal of the American Medical Association, 223*, 257-259.

International classification of diseases: Clinical modifications (9th rev.) (1980). Ann Arbor, MI: Commission of Professional and Hospital Activities.

U.S. Department of Health and Human Services, Bureau of Health Care Delivery and Assistance. (September, 1982). *Clinical data collection and retrieval systems for small primary care projects.* Rockville, MD: Administrative Publication, 4-5.

Weed, L. L. (1969). *Medical records, medical education and patient care.* Cleveland, OH: The Press of Case Western Reserve University.

FURTHER READING

Eimerl, T. S. (1960). Organized curiosity. *Journal of College of General Practitioners, 3*, 246-52.

Family Practice Recertification. (1962, April). *Journal of Family Practice, 4*, 22-23, 27, 31-32, 41, 137, 141, 145-147.

Farley, E. S., Boisseau, V., & Froom, J. (1977). An integrated medical record and data system for primary care. Part 5: Implications of filing family folders by area of residence. *Journal of Family Practice, 5*(3), 427-32.

Farley, E. S., & Treat, D. F. (1973). Utilization of community resources. In H. F. Conn, R. E. Rakel, & T. W. Johnson (Eds.), *Family practice.* Philadelphia: W. B. Saunders.

Froom, J. (1977). An integrated medical record and data system for primary care. Part 1: The age/sex register: Definition of the patient population. *Journal of Family Practice, 4*(5), 951-953.

Froom, J. (1977). An integrated medical record and data system for primary care. Part 2: Classification of health problems for use by family physicians. *Journal of Family Practice, 4*(6), 1149-51.

Froom, J., Culpepper, L., & Boisseau, V. (1977). An integrated medical record and data system for primary care. Part 3: The diagnostic index manual and computer methods and applications. *Journal of Family Practice, 5*, 113-120.

Froom, J., Culpepper, L., & Kirkwood, C. R. (1977). An integrated medical record and data system for primary care. Part 4: Family information. *Journal of Family Practice, 5*(2), 265-70.

Froom, J., Culpepper, L., & Kirkwood, C. R. (1977). An integrated medical record and data system for primary care. Part 7: The encounter form: Problems and prospects for a universal type. *Journal of Family Practice, 5*(5), 845-49.

International classification of health problems in primary care (2nd ed.). (1979). Oxford: Oxford University Press.

Minnesota Systems Research, Inc. (1977). *Classification and codes for children and youth — social work.* DHEW Training Grant No. MCT-001036-02.

Chapter 9

INTERPROFESSIONAL COLLABORATION

Carl G. Leukefeld
Robert J. Battjes

Social workers in the primary care team provide necessary and valuable services that are essential to the patient's well-being. In the present cost-conscious environment, social work must be able to demonstrate that it provides cost-effective services that meet patient needs. To demonstrate the value of its services, social work must first clearly establish its role within primary health care. As Rossen (1987) suggests, the key to social work's future in hospitals and other primary care settings is the profession's ability to articulate its role within the context of change.

The purpose of this chapter is to review social work's role in primary health care as an integral part of the health care team. After considering challenges to interdisciplinary collaboration identified by the Joint Commission on Interprofessional Affairs (JCIA), the emergence of the interdisciplinary team in primary care is addressed. Role expectation and conflicts are briefly reviewed and examined, and factors that facilitate team development are considered. The chapter concludes with brief remarks related to social work and the health care team.

NOTE: This chapter was prepared by government employees as part of their official duties; therefore, the material is in the public domain and may be reproduced or copied without permission.

PROFESSIONAL ROLES AND
RESPONSIBILITIES

Guidelines developed by the Joint Commission on Interprofessional Affairs (1986a) for the mental health field provide a useful framework for examining professional roles and responsibilities in primary health care. The JCIA was founded in 1974 with representatives from the American Nurses Association, the American Psychiatric Association, the American Psychological Association, and the National Association of Social Workers. The Commission developed guidelines to increase interprofessional respect, trust, and cooperation.

The transmittal memorandum for the guidelines succinctly outlines the challenges of interdisciplinary collaboration, with the following rationale:

> Role relationships and boundaries that are unclear or a cause of conflict, can frustrate efforts to devise optimally effective services. It was a recognition of these critical circumstances that prompted the JCIA to develop a set of *Guidelines* which could encompass a common set of understandings (definitions and descriptions) concerning interprofessional roles and relationships in the mental health field. . . . The *Guidelines* do not propose solutions to conflict, to role overlapping and blurring or to unclear official mandates. Nor do they address existing and continuing debates regarding the efficacy of various clinical approaches. Rather, they seek to encourage healthy, and hopefully, productive dialogue. . . .
>
> It is essential that agencies, facilities and other entities promote the clarification of roles and role boundaries, and their inter-relationships. These *Guidelines* endeavor to aid the process of collaboration, to assist in conflict resolution. They represent the desire to keep sound patient/client care as the goal of inter-professional efforts. (JCIA, 1986b)

The Guidelines themselves further suggest factors that hinder collaboration:

> Each of the professions has developed its own unique identity based on a separate history. Since the scope of practice of each overlaps with the others, competitive conditions exist which may result in mistrust, conflict, and mutually destructive interaction. Moreover, the history and traditions of each of the disciplines have produced certain conceptual and language systems by which each operates. Although there are many similarities in these systems, a lack of standardization of definition of commonly used terms has contributed to many of the disagreements that occur between the professions. (JCIA, 1986a, p. 1).

Role conflict is not unique to the mental health field and might also be a significant factor in all interdisciplinary settings. Thus, as the JCIA Guidelines indicate, there is a need to recognize and deal with conflict in interdisciplinary primary care settings. To do so, it is useful to review the emergence of the interdisciplinary approach.

THE EMERGENCE OF THE INTERDISCIPLINARY TEAM APPROACH

The impetus for interdisciplinary teams in health care has been attributed to the community mental health center movement in the mid-1960s (Harris, Saunders, & Zasorin-Connors, 1978). The emergence of interdisciplinary teams in primary care followed shortly thereafter, with reports of such teams in community health centers in the late 1960s (Banta & Fox, 1972). In the 1970s increasing emphasis was placed on the use of interdisciplinary teams in primary health care, and this emphasis has continued into the 1980s. The interdisciplinary team has since been used widely in a variety of primary health care settings. Interdisciplinary teamwork has been identified as the most frequently used approach to organize and unify health care delivery (Lowe & Herranen, 1981). Miller (1987) and Rossen (1987) indicated that the interdisciplinary team is essential to accomplish the goals of primary care.

The reason for this emphasis on the interdisciplinary team has been explained from several points of view. According to Lowe and Herranen (1981), specialization within the health care field requires coordination of individuals with varied expertise for appropriate patient care. Harris et al. (1978) note that patients and their families need a range of services requiring various skills, and the team approach can promote service coordination and avoid duplication. Ducanis and Golin (1979) suggest that the interdisciplinary team approach is based on the assumption that the team brings together diverse skills and expertise to provide higher quality service. They identify three factors influential in the emergence of the interdisciplinary team approach: 1) the concept of the "whole" patient; that is, recognition that the various problems of a patient are interrelated and must be addressed in a coordinated manner; 2) organization that clarifies lines of communication and authority to avoid fragmentation; and 3) external mandates regarding quality of care and accountability. Another factor was the emphasis on a "systems approach."

Miller (1987) suggests that the team approach fits a systems perspective in which health providers with various expertise offer services, monitor patient movement, plan for community support, and interact to respond to the community and residents. Also, the movement toward "comprehensive" health care rather than medical care requires an integration of social and medical problems, resulting in a need for increased collaboration (see, for example, Rubin & Beckhard, 1972).

Despite the emphasis on interdisciplinary teams, Lowe and Herranen (1981) note that

> . . . considerable confusion surrounds the concept of teamwork. Teamwork evokes multiple, automatic and dissimilar responses in all professionals. To some, the word teamwork is synonymous with collaboration, to others with any group action. Many view teamwork as beneficial to patient care while others perceive teamwork as further fragmenting care . . . . (p. 1)

It is important to define the term "interdisciplinary team." Ducanis and Golin (1979) define the interdisciplinary team as "a functioning unit, composed of individuals with varied and specialized training, who coordinate their activities to provide services to a client or group of clients" (p. 3). Key to this definition is the term "functioning unit." Ducanis and Golin emphasize that the involvement of multiple professions does not assure a team approach. Kane (1982, p. 2) provides another definition: "a small working group with a commonly espoused purpose, differentiated roles, and ongoing communication processes."

Although the interdisciplinary team approach in primary health care is widely espoused, implementation of the ideal is not without problems. Kane (1982) refers to social work's preoccupation with the team approach as a love-hate relationship, a cherished ideal, yet a constant frustration. She reports on a survey of *Health and Social Work* readers who "were practically unanimous in citing the exigencies of multidisciplinary team practice and the associated juggling of complex role relationships as the most distinctive feature of social work practice in a health care setting" (p.2).

Kane (1982) also identifies three sources of ineffective teamwork: lack of a clearly stated, shared, and measurable purpose; lack of clearly defined roles for team members; and lack of an appropriate mechanism for the timely exchange of information. Elsewhere, Kane (1975) noted the absence of a planned decision-making process as a common problem of interprofessional teams.

Ducanis and Golin (1979) also identify barriers to interdisciplinary team development. Barriers include lack of awareness of team members' skills; sense of autonomy developed in professional training; differences in ethical codes; lack of common goals; communication barriers resulting from lack of time, space, and differences in professional jargon; and ambiguous and overlapping roles.

ROLE EXPECTATIONS AND CONFLICT

Of all the barriers to interdisciplinary collaboration, problems that stem from role confusion or role conflict appear primary. Rossen (1987) suggests that medical environments, unlike nonmedical social work settings, are centers of multidisciplinary practice characterized by role confusion. Olsen and Olsen (1967) note that the roles of social workers within medical settings are complex and vaguely defined because social work services must be highly coordinated with many other services. They identify three factors that contribute to role confusion:

1) social work is an ancillary service in a host setting;
2) the social workers must operate as part of a professional team; and
3) social work practice must always take account of the dominant authority of the physician. (Olsen & Olsen, 1967, p. 70)

Olsen and Olsen (1967) note also that the diverse professionals constituting teams in medical settings inevitably hold different expectations regarding team roles of various professions. Similarly, Ducanis and Golin (1979) point out that professionals often are not clearly aware of the competencies and roles of other professions. "Overlapping roles, status differences, and differences in viewpoint can easily lead to interprofessional conflict and thus create discord within the team" (Ducanis & Golin, 1979, p. 31).

In their study of physician and social worker role expectations, Olsen and Olsen (1967) found that:

A considerable amount of conflict did exist between the physicians and social workers both in expectations for and perceptions of the social worker role. Physicians . . . were willing to grant considerably fewer professional responsibilities to social workers than these social workers thought they should have . . . . (p. 78)

Lister (1980) studied the role expectations of health professionals by surveying 13 professional groups. He found considerable overlap in the roles of the various professions. Specifically, he noted "the lack of clarity and specificity of the social worker's role. On no item in the study were social workers and all others in agreement that the task was primarily the social worker's" (p. 49). He did report agreement among physicians, social workers, and nurses regarding social work's role in making posthospital care referrals. Many other roles that social workers assigned to themselves, however, often were assigned also to other professions. Helping patients with emotional problems, for example, was assigned often to clergy, nurses, and social workers, while providing continued contact with patients and family was seen by the majority of physicians and clergy as a task of their own professions.

In a community health center study, Banta and Fox (1972) found divergence in role expectation to be one source of role conflict. Other staff expected social workers to help patients find financial assistance whereas the social workers saw their role as teaching patients to help themselves. Difference in professional orientation was also a major source of role conflict, with the approaches of social workers and public health nurses being quite different. For example,

> The nurses defined their role and their relationship to patients in a more diffuse, active, directive and supportive way than social workers did. Social workers thought it important to select clients and problems with foresight as to whether they could offer some real help. They believed in setting limited, "realistic" goals with clients, whom they would guide or counsel but whom they would not overbearingly or maternalistically direct. . . . they thought that [empathy] ought to be tempered with a greater modicum of detachment and objectivity than the nurses did. (Banta & Fox, 1972, p. 719)

In a study of health care professionals from various disciplines, Ducanis and Golin (1979) documented role overlap. Over half the sample indicated that physicians, nurses, and social workers infringed on their territory, and most did not believe that their capabilities were fully used by other professionals.

Interprofessional conflict not only emerges within health care settings but also was found by Harris et al. (1978) among the faculty of an interdisciplinary educational program for students in various professional programs. They observed that

Conflicts arose between faculty members from various disciplines, particularly among nurses and social workers. . . . They frequently reflected the differences in the ways professionals in each discipline approach practice. Physicians generally assume a management model that stresses cause and effect relationships; nurses put more emphasis on education and, therefore, stress the communication of information; and social workers emphasize a helping model that stresses the use of the relationship to assist clients to gain understanding and insight. (p. 49)

INTERDISCIPLINARY TEAM DEVELOPMENT

Lowe and Herranen (1981) observed that teamwork is an evolutionary process. In the process of evolution, the team progresses through a series of stages in which role ambiguity and role conflict emerge; roles and responsibilities are defined and clarified; and communication, decision-making and leadership patterns are developed. Its final stage, "team maintenance,"

. . . is characterized by shared acknowledgment of team tasks. . . . There now exists an awareness that multiple variables influence the group's efforts to work together to manage their independence. . . . Team members have a thorough understanding of their own special input as well as knowledge and recognition of the skills of other team members. . . . Team leadership is more flexible. . . . the actual leadership role shifts to the person best equipped for carrying out the client care plan. . . . Members recognize and value the viewpoints of other disciplines: compromise and negotiation occur in setting priorities and on redirecting the analysis of complex issues. . . . Role conflict is dealt with by jointly clarifying expectations, identifying competences, evaluating overlapping functions and negotiating assignments. (pp. 4-5)

According to Beckhard (1972), the team needs to spend time during its early development considering how its members will work together. This planning should include the specific role definition of each member, members' role expectations, issues that need to be dealt with by the team as a whole, the members' information needs, and how the flow of communications and information can be facilitated. Beckhard (1972) also emphasizes the importance of clarifying roles, especially in community settings where roles are often poorly defined. He recommends the development of "living" rather than formal job descriptions. Thus, team members describe what they do in writing and then validate these descriptions with other team members. Beckhard underscores the importance of communication. He recommends that the communications process be analyzed not only to determine what information needs to be shared and who needs to know what but also to clarify communication paths among organizational components.

Rubin and Beckhard (1972) stress the importance of a conscious process to help team members consider "goals, tasks, relationships, decision-making, norms, backgrounds and values" (p. 332). Team members should be involved as both participants and observers in this process. Training is needed for the entire team as a unit, for some members to develop leadership skills, and for the socialization of new members. For the total team, they recommend an "action planning" process that includes:

1. Assign priorities to the multiple issues . . .;
2. Decide upon the most appropriate format to use (total group, homogeneous versus heterogeneous subgroups, and so forth) to generate solutions or alternatives;
3. Develop a clear and shared set of change objectives or goals . . .;
4. Allocate individual and subgroup responsibilities to implement chosen actions;
5. Specify mechanisms and procedures for checking progress (follow-up). (p. 330)

Ducanis and Golin (1979) also emphasize that professionals need to be trained to function as part of a team, which requires a conscious program of team development. This process should be planned and orderly, and a normal part of team functioning. As part of this developmental process, team members need to become familiar with each other's skills; clarify the boundaries of each other's responsibilities; clarify perceptions and expectations regarding each other's roles; interpret their professions' ethical codes to each other; clarify team goals (using goal definition exercises to uncover hidden conflicts); and clarify communications patterns. Ducanis and Golin further recommend a problem-solving approach to conflict management that includes four steps: identification of the conflict; exploration of solutions; testing a solution; and evaluating the results.

Recognizing the importance of preparing students for teamwork during professional training, Harris et al. (1978) designed a program to assist students from various health care disciplines develop skills in effective team participation. The course focused on understanding other health disciplines, skills in communicating and problem-solving with other disciplines, skills in working within groups, and skills in using community resources. In addition, students developed a commitment to patients rather than to specific health problems, they learned to encourage patients and families to accept some responsibility for health problems and health care, and they recognized that many family and community factors affect health. Using this content, the educational program was found to increase professional interaction and willingness to use other professionals and community resources.

While the importance of the interdisciplinary team approach has been widely recognized, Kane (1982) suggests the need to reevaluate the use of such teams. Effective teamwork is a time-consuming, expensive process that should be used only when clearly needed. It should be used "when substantial sustained interaction among caregivers is really required to achieve specific measurable goals. . . . Let us not confuse the need for an array of multidisciplinary services with the need for team delivery" (pp. 3-4).

THE SOCIAL WORK ROLE

Considering the role confusion and overlap in the primary care team, it is reasonable to ask: What is social work's role? As a first step, identifying social work's objectives will identify the profession's role within the primary health care team. Berkman (1978) suggests eight professional objectives for social work in health. (She also referred to authors who have written in each of these eight areas.) Five of the objectives she identified are related directly to patient care and can help clarify social work objectives and roles. Berkman's five selected objectives are:

1. To assess the psychosocial and environmental stresses that physically ill persons and their families may encounter and to provide direct therapeutic help.
2. To assist patients and families in optimum use of social-health care programs.
3. To make appropriate social health care and prevention programs available and accessible to all patients in need.
4. To socialize and humanize the institutional program in the interest of patient needs.
5. To contribute to comprehensive treatment of the patient by collaborating with the physician and other personnel involved.

It is important also to define social work clearly in order to clarify social work's role and unique identity as part of the primary health care team. Social work is defined as:

> . . . the professional activity of helping individuals, groups, or communities improve their social functioning and creating societal conditions favorable to this goal. It can be described further as consisting of the professional application of social work values, principles, and techniques to one or more of the following ends: helping people obtain tangible services; providing counseling and psychotherapy to individuals, families, and groups; helping communities or groups provide or improve social and health services; and participating in relevant policymaking forums. The practice of social work requires knowledge of human development and behavior; of social, economic, and cultural institutions; and of the interaction of all these factors. (Congressional Record, 1986)

More specifically and for medical settings, the National Association of Social Workers' Clinical Council has defined social work as

> . . . the professional application of social work practice, theories and methods in the treatment of mental and emotional conditions and in the maintenance and enhancement of psychosocial functioning of individuals, families and small groups.
>
> Clinical social work embraces treatment directed to interpersonal interactions, intrapsychic dynamics, life support, and management issues. The principle of person-in-situation is central to all clinical understanding and action. Clinical social work is undertaken within the principles in the Code of Ethics for the social work profession.
>
> Clinical social work services include assessment, diagnosis, and a range of other interventions including psychotherapy. These services are designed to: a) alleviate psychopathology through the modification of dysfunctional behavior and/or symptom removal; b) modify psychosocial conditions which affect individuals or groups of individuals with respect to behavior, emotions and thinking as these relate to their intrapersonal and interpersonal processes; and c) assist patients to maintain or improve life situations threatened or affected by social and psychological stress or ill health. (Council on Clinical Social Work, 1983, p. 1)

Much of the attention given to the role of social work in health care settings applies to its role in primary care. Admission to health care for many patients is a time of crisis requiring psychosocial as well as direct monetary and other assistance. Saxton and Dunn (1983) note, for example, that hospital admission may produce numerous responses or problems requiring social work intervention. Typical problems include anxiety, depression, anger, financial and sexual concerns, grief (related to loss of function, body part, or death), and need for posthospitalization referrals (rehabilitation, skilled nursing, meals-on-wheels, therapy, and others). Humble (1984) identifies social work's role in the health care team as intake evaluation, social crisis intervention, discharge planning, supportive services, and counseling. Miller and Rehr (1983) suggest that social work practice in hospitals is varied and includes: 1) early patient case findings to identify stressful situations and problems; 2) interpreting the meaning of shared information with patients and their families for decision-making; 3) mediating and coordinating medical care projects with the patient and practitioner; 4) working for social-environmental changes to safeguard the continuation of services to the patient; 5) early and appropriate discharge planning; and 6) adhering to requirements for reimbursement.

AN EXAMPLE OF TEAM COLLABORATION

Mary J. is an eighteen-year-old single woman who contacted the community health center for assistance with her first pregnancy. She lives at home with her parents in a low-income section of a large metropolitan city. Mary J. is in her senior year of high school and works part-time at a local fast-food restaurant.

Mary J. fainted during a physical education class at school, and following a brief evaluation by the school nurse, was referred to the health center. At the center, Mary J. was initially evaluated by Ms. N., a nurse-health educator, who gathered initial medical and social history information. Mary J. was then examined by Dr. P., who made an appointment for a follow-up visit. After her initial visit and receipt of laboratory results, Mary J.'s case was reviewed by the health care team, consisting of Dr. P., Mr. N., Ms. H., the team health care aide, and Ms. S., the social work consultant to the team. (Note: Because of recent funding cutbacks, the number of health center social workers has been reduced, and social workers are now working across teams, primarily as consultants to other team members.)

During the team meeting, several problems emerged as Dr. P. and Ms. N. presented their assessments of Mary J.:

> Mary J. appears to be four months pregnant and has received no prenatal care; her diet is inadequate; she has not told her parents or her boyfriend

that she is pregnant and has no definite plans for her baby; she admits to daily use of alcohol and marijuana and occasional use of cocaine.

The team developed a preliminary treatment plan, including regular prenatal care appointments with Dr. P., enrollment in prenatal/nutrition classes with Ms. N., and psychosocial history and assessment with Ms. S. Based on her preliminary assessment, Ms. N. thought Mary J. would probably need close supervision during the course of treatment and suggested that Ms. S. determine the need for ongoing involvement by Ms. H.

Mary J. failed to keep her follow-up appointment. Since Dr. P. had established rapport with her during the initial visit, he contacted Mary J. and made another appointment. During the second clinic visit, she agreed to a schedule of regular clinic appointments and enrollment in a five-week prenatal/nutrition class. During her interview with Ms. S., Mary J. indicated concern about telling her parents and boyfriend that she was pregnant, ambivalence regarding what she would do with the baby, and a desire to stop using alcohol and drugs during her pregnancy. Ms. S. agreed to meet with Mary J. and her parents and also with Mary J. and her boyfriend. Ms. S. and Mary J. developed a five-week psychosocial treatment plan to deal with Mary's confusion about her pregnancy and plans for the baby. Ms. S. referred Mary J. to the local chemical dependency program for substance abuse treatment. Also, recognizing that Mary J. would require considerable support and assistance in following through on her clinic treatment plan, Ms. S. introduced her to Ms. H., who would serve as Mary's case manager.

Following the second appointment, the team again reviewed Mary J.'s treatment plan, and incorporated Ms. S.'s psychosocial treatment assessment into the team plan. The team also confirmed the designation of Ms. H. as case manager, with responsibility for regular clinic contact with Mary J., outreach to Mary J. if appointments are missed, and liaison with the chemical dependency program.

The purpose of this case is not to complete the story of Mary J., but to depict role overlap and ambiguity within the treatment team and how this is effectively and efficiently handled by an integrated team. Because of the shortage of social workers in the clinic, the nurse, Ms. N., had been designated to fulfill a traditional social work function: conducting an initial psychosocial assessment. Yet, the social worker was still involved as a consultant in treatment planning. Because the initial assessment indicated that major psychosocial treatment issues existed, direct involvement of the social worker was easily incorporated. The physician, Dr. P., departed from his normal role, in contacting Mary J. when she failed to keep her second appointment, demonstrating the need for flexibility in role assignment based not only on expertise, but also on special circumstances.

Efficient and effective teamwork requires that team members have authority to implement independently components of the treatment plan without waiting for the next team review. Thus, Ms. S. implemented the psychosocial treatment plan and referral to substance abuse treatment, reporting back to the team after the fact. Similarly, she implemented tentative plans to involve Ms. H. as case manager, without discussing this action with the team.

What this case of Mary J. depicts is that four health professionals representing different perspectives can jointly deliver an integrated program of care. Together they can work interdependently, with each member having autonomy within the framework established by the team. Through mutual agreement and negotiation, team roles are established, and these roles are altered according to the needs of the patient and the realities of the institution.

CONCLUDING REMARKS

For the various reasons presented in this chapter, it appears that the interdisciplinary health care team will continue to be a significant factor in primary care. Primary care settings by nature are interdisciplinary, which makes coordinated decision-making and patient care planning so vital. The interdisciplinary team provides essential interaction for patient care. Currently, there is no substitute for this important coordinating function. Traditionally, the medical record progress note has served as a tool for information-sharing among team members. Perhaps new technologies such as interacting computer programs are on the horizon, but they are not yet viable alternatives.

This chapter has identified both the strengths of and constraints to effective interdisciplinary team functioning in primary care. Role conflict and confusion are presented as key constraints. In order to maximize their effectiveness within the primary health care team, social workers must clearly delineate their role and must periodically reassess and reclarify social work functions.

In addition to clarifying social work's own role in the primary health care team, it is suggested here that social workers with the traditional focus on the person-in-environment are uniquely qualified to facilitate cooperation within the primary care team. Social work facilitation can maintain the openness necessary to negotiate roles and procedures and to serve as an advocate for the individual patient—a value highly regarded by the social work tradition.

Finally, the literature reviewed in this chapter revealed a paucity of research studies that focus on the interdisciplinary team. Most of the literature is descriptive and anecdotal. The research that has been conducted has focused on identifying problems in the implementation of the team approach, but has not posited or tested possible solutions to these problems. Considering the importance of the interdisciplinary approach to primary health care and the lack of research to guide effective interdisciplinary practice, it appears that the interdisciplinary team is a fruitful area for social work research.

REFERENCES

Banta, H. D., & Fox, R. C. (1972). Role strains of a health care team in a poverty community. *Social Science and Medicine, 6,* 697-722.

Beckhard, R. (1972). Organizational issues in the team delivery of comprehensive health care. *The Milbank Memorial Fund Quarterly, 5,* 287-36.

Berkman, B. (1978). *Knowledge base and program needs for effective social work practice in health: A review of the literature.* Chicago, IL: Society for Hospital Social Work Directors of the American Hospital Association.

Congressional Record. (1986). 99th Congress, 132: 18, February 25, 1986.

Council on Clinical Social Work. (1983). *Definition of clinical social work.* Silver Spring, MD: National Association of Social Workers.

Ducanis, A. J., & Golin, A. K. (1979). *The interdisciplinary health care team: A handbook.* Germantown, MD: Aspen Systems Corporation.

Harris, J. L., Saunders, D. N., & Zasorin-Connors, J. (1978). A training program for interprofessional health care teams. *Health and Social Work, 3,* 36-53.

Humble, J. (1984, July). The social worker's importance on the health care team. *Texas Hospitals,* 32-34.

Joint Commission on Interprofessional Affairs (JCIA). (1986a). *Guidelines for interprofessional relations in the mental health field.* Silver Springs, MD: The National Association of Social Workers.

Joint Commission on Interprofessional Affairs (JCIA). (1986b). *Trasmittal memorandum to the guidelines on discharge planning.* Silver Spring, MD: National Association of Social Workers.

Kane, R. (1975). The interprofessional team as a small group. *Social Work in Health Care, 1,* 19-32.

Kane, R. (1982). Teams: Thoughts from the bleachers. *Health and Social Work, 7*(2), 2-4.

Lister, L. (1980). Role expectation of social workers and other health professionals. *Health and Social Work, 5,* 41-49.

Lowe, J. I., & Herranen, M. (1981). Understanding teamwork: Another look at the concepts. *Social Work in Health Care, 7,* 1-11.

Miller, R. (1987). Primary health care. In A. Minahan (Ed.), *Encyclopedia of social work* (18th ed. Vol. 2). Silver Spring, MD: National Association of Social Workers, 2, 321-324.

Miller, R. S., & Rehr, H. (1983). Health settings and health providers. In R. S. Miller & H. Rehr (Eds.), *Social work issues in health care.* Englewood Cliffs, NJ: Prentice-Hall.

Olsen, K. M., & Olsen, M. E. (1967). Role expectations and perceptions for social workers in medical settings. *Social Work,* July, 70-78.

Rossen, S. (1987). Hospital social work. In A. Minahan (Ed.), *Encyclopedia of social work* (18th ed. Vol. 1). Silver Spring, MD: National Association of Social Workers, 1, 816-821.

Rubin, I. M., & Beckhard, R. (1972). Factors influencing the effectiveness of health teams. *The Milbank Memorial Fund Quarterly, 5,* 317-335.

Saxton, P. M., & Dunn, M. (1983). *The place of clinical social work in reimbursement for health care services.* Sacramento, CA: National Association of Social Workers, California Chapter, Committee on Health Care Financing.

FURTHER READING

Berkman, B. (1974). Editorial: Social work and the challenge of DRGs. *Health and Social Work, 9*(1), 2-3.

Berkman, B. (1987). Health care specialization. In A. Minahan (Ed.), *Encyclopedia of social work* (18th ed., Vol. 1). Silver Spring, MD: National Association of Social Workers, *1,* 710-714.

Chapter 10

THE ADMINISTRATOR'S PERSPECTIVE

Ronald W. Kemp

Most administrators do not need to be convinced that adding social work services would significantly enhance the scope and quality of services in primary care settings, particularly if they have completed an assessment of patient needs. Unfortunately, a similar assessment of reimbursement systems clearly demonstrates to them that this component could not be financially self-sufficient. Although these financial barriers exist, many publicly-sponsored primary care settings have moved ahead and added social work services to meet the needs of patients, to reduce the amount of time and energy physicians and administrators spend resolving psychosocial problems, and to address state and federal requirements and guidelines. Hospitals and health maintenance organizations (HMOs) have also added social workers because of these reasons and to be competitive in the marketplace. Although HMOs, hospitals, and publicly sponsored primary care programs have funding mechanisms that are sufficiently flexible to allow the employment of social workers, private for-profit group practices are not in the same position. A for-profit group practice could only justify this type of cost if it were very large (5 to 10 physicians) or if the role were confined to providing mental health counseling to patients who could afford to pay for the service.

Social work services could be more fully utilized if administrators and providers in primary care settings clearly understood the variety of roles social workers can play in this type of setting. It is hoped that this chapter will stimulate private and public primary care centers to examine the potential for employing social work professionals. The previous chapters have outlined each of these roles in detail. The administrator's role is to help with the decision regarding the specific role that is needed for his/her particular setting.

As patients' and society's expectations of the health care society system change to require more comprehensive care, it will become apparent that the delivery of primary care no longer can be accomplished by the physician alone. Support services provided by other professionals will be needed to accomplish this task. The expansion of social work services in primary care will occur to the extent that they are needed when reimbursement becomes common among third- party health insurance programs. Expansion of social work services could occur if physicians and administrators would develop a better understanding of the contribution that social workers could make to improve the quality of care, reduce total health care cost, or to increase physician productivity.

Administrators of primary care centers are influenced by internal and external interest groups, funding sources, market-place pressures, and professional/medical review organizations. Internally, physicians' needs, nursing staff expectations, patient demographics, and budgetary constraints also influence the administrator's planning and decision-making. Administrators should base their decisions regarding the development of a social work component on objective and subjective information and a formal planning process that includes the following:

Developing a Plan: Do the needs of the patients and the setting require social work services? What changes would be expected by other personnel if a social work component were developed for the setting? How are other primary care settings attempting to solve their patients' psychosocial problems?

Deciding a Specific Social Work Role: What specific tasks will the professional social worker be required to perform? Who will be involved in the planning of tasks? How will the tasks be prioritized?

Developing a Recruitment Strategy: What type of social work professional would best meet the setting's needs? Who should be consulted regarding recruitment? Where should the setting advertise? What credentials should applicants have? Who should perform the interview when nobody on staff is a social worker? What type of compensation plan is needed to attract a qualified social worker?

Establishing Evaluation Criteria: How does the setting evaluate the success of the position? How is the value of the position to be separated from the performance of the person? What are the objective measures used to evaluate the social work position? Who will evaluate and supervise the social worker?

If this planning process is used, problems and misunderstandings for the social worker, other providers, and the administrator will be minimized.

PLANNING

Planning should be objective, follow a logical path, and should involve as many key staff personnel as possible. The process should include:

1. A search of the literature. (Journals that are recommended are *Health and Social Work, Journal of Ambulatory Care Management, The Health Care Supervisor*, and *Health Care Management*.)
2. A survey of patient needs. These could include random surveys of patients using the center, staff regarding patient needs, and collateral agencies used by the center's patients.
3. A survey of other primary care settings that already have a social work component.

Regardless of the structure of the primary center, administrators need to involve key staff in the assessment process to generate enthusiasm and support for the position and to provide informal and formal information to assist in the decision. Because staff that are actually providing the direct services to the patients are in the best position to identify the psychosocial needs of patients, they should be appointed to a search committee to select the social worker.

Literature search. Staff should then review the literature. Administrators should begin by providing key staff with journal articles and other documents related to social work in primary care and health care in general. The Nursing Supervisor and Medical Director are the most likely candidates to review various articles and participate in the search committee.

Patient surveys. Administrators can take a number of approaches in surveying patient needs. The most useful surveys involve an analysis of demographic and diagnostic data on patients. These surveys will provide information on the frequency of various illnesses among patients, and the age and sex of the patient population. Patient surveys also can involve interviews with nursing staff and physicians that will identify patients who may need social services (e.g., patients who are resistant to treatment for life-threatening illnesses, patients who repeatedly seek treatment for substance abuse, depressed patients who are reluctant to seek counseling) and health care needs such as dental and optometry that are not generally available to patients of the center.

Direct patient surveys can yield data that may reinforce the need for social work services. These surveys must be developed carefully so that valid and reliable data are obtained. The best approach is to have nursing staff randomly interview patients coming to the center and being seen by the physician. The administrator should be actively involved in preparing such patient interviews.

Surveys of other primary care settings. The process should begin by surveying other primary care settings either locally or nationally in order to get the perspectives of other administrators. A list of such settings can be obtained from state health departments, universities, national associations of community health centers, and state medical societies. Schools of social work and public health can also help identify primary care programs that have social work components.

CLARIFICATION OF ROLES

The decision to employ a social worker within the primary care setting requires careful evaluation and planning. Because the social worker is unlikely to generate revenue, employment is based on the need of the center to provide more comprehensive and higher quality of care, or because such services are required by funding sources.

Although many primary care settings offering social work services have been tax-supported medical or health programs serving low-income populations, it would be unfair to conclude that the value of social work services is limited to these types of primary care setting centers. Along with the growing emphasis on primary care and preventive medicine, we have seen an increased awareness of social, cultural, and economic conditions that affect the health of patients. The relationship between diet, stress, and emotions to cardiovascular diseases, ulcers, colitis, allergies, and other conditions is apparent. On the other hand, illness disrupts the personal or family equilibrium and may hinder the patient's coping abilities. These social and emotional upheavals then feed back into the individual's recovery or well-being. Maintaining health requires a variety of interventions. No longer can we simply identify the technical pathology and prescribe treatment. Financial issues have forced administrators to reevaluate the ways they should provide health care. This broader concept has increased the importance of a variety of other health service professionals (social workers, home health aides, nutritionists, public health nurses, and others) who facilitate the effective use of medical resources. Costs can be reduced by these supportive professionals when the total treatment plan is effective, and hospitals, nursing homes, and physicians are appropriately utilized.

Technology and cognitive requirements of modern medicine have required primary care physicians to be more specialized. Because of these changes and the renewed philosophy of the comprehensive medical practice, additional health professionals with specialized training will also be needed to provide services to patients. Clinical nutritionists, health educators, and social workers have critical roles to play in primary care settings.

Employment of a professional social worker should:

1. Increase compliance with treatment plans
2. Increase the effectiveness of treatment plans by improved communication with the patient's family and natural support systems
3. Reduce interference with medical treatment plans through earlier intervention into patient's emotional dysfunctioning and/or substance abuse
4. Improve treatment outcome through improved communication with referral organizations
5. Improve professional staff understanding of complexities of individual patient behavior and their ability to solve psychosocial problems
6. Provide in-service training to staff
7. Develop health promotion/disease prevention programs
8. Provide counseling to patients with emotional and family problems
9. Improve linkages with categorical community resources.

Specific roles and skills are required to accomplish these goals. It is essential for the administrator to evaluate the needs of the setting and to decide which role is most essential. The introduction found in this book clarifies how these priorities could be established. In turn, the qualifications and experience of the social worker must be compatible with the setting's and the patients' needs.

Bracht (1977), in a paper on social work in health care, lists five premises underlying social work practice in health settings:

1. Social, cultural, and economic conditions have a significant and measurable effect on both a) health status and b) illness prevention and recovery. Research increasingly suggests positive relationships between these variables and the process an illness takes.
2. Illness-related behaviors, whether perceived or actual, frequently disrupt personal and family equilibrium and coping abilities. Illness conditions, whether acute, chronic or terminal, can be exacerbated by the effects of treatment.
3. Medical treatment alone is often incomplete, and occasionally impossible to render, without accompanying social support and counseling services.
4. Problems in access to and appropriate use of health services are sufficiently severe to require concerted action.
5. Multiprofessional health team collaboration on selected individual and community health problems is an effective approach to solving complex socio-medical problems.

Bracht discussed the validity of each of these premises and referenced sociological, behavioral, and social work literature that documents recent research that supports each premise.

Social work practice in hospitals, clinics, or other medical facilities contributes to the total care of the patient through helping the patient or his family with social and emotional problems that frequently exist or arise in connection with illness. This help often amounts to assisting patients or their families to look more objectively at choices. It involves developing an environment in which insight might be strengthened, and frequently it provides the outside assistance in setting priorities relating to health issues. This intervention provides the potential for patients to derive the maximum benefit from medical care and rehabilitation services.

The social worker in a medical setting works as a member of a team that can include the physician, nurse, nutritionist, health educator, and all other professional personnel who contribute to the care of the individual patients. It is the responsibility of the social worker to obtain information about a patient's social situation and adjustment as is pertinent to the physician's understanding and treatment of the illness. It is also the medical social worker's role to help the patient and his family understand, accept, and use medical recommendations. This implies working toward the removal of environmental and emotional obstacles that impede the patient's recovery, and helping individuals and families adjust to circumstances changed because of prolonged or disabling illnesses.

According to Hirsch and Lurie (1969), social workers have a responsibility for leadership especially in the areas of prevention and rehabilitation. This has developed partly because of the expertise and tradition of the profession:

> Social work is steeped in the health of the individual rather than in his pathology. The training of social workers is geared toward helping to prevent breakdown in social functioning by reinforcing the ego strengths and resources of the individual. Creativity and innovation in the prevention of social dysfunctioning and in promoting rehabilitation are the hallmark of social work. (Hirsch & Lurie, 1969, p. 20)

A social worker would be a useful addition to the center's medical team by fulfilling the need of other providers for in-service education. Also, by having a social work component, more effective communications can be developed with community agencies.

RECRUITMENT

Social work practice within the primary care setting requires specific skills and interest. Administrators cannot assume that any social worker will be equally effective in this type of practice. A review of the potential employee's personality traits, educational background, and employment history is an absolute requirement. The results of the needs assessment process should also be taken into account when making a final selection.

The social work profile can be divided into four areas: personality factors, educational background, social work employment experience, primary care/medical and work experience.

Certain personality factors lend themselves to performance of social work practice in primary care organizations.

Flexibility. Primary care settings offer a variety of intervention opportunities:

- mental health assessments
- support groups
- marital dysfunctioning
- abuse and neglect intervention

— substance abuse
— advocacy with other service agencies
— financial counseling
— child care techniques

Flexibility includes not only the ability to intervene in quite different types of presenting problems but also the willingness and need to succeed professionally within each type.

Confidence. Success of social work intervention requires confidence and specific knowledge. Although confidence comes from an array of maturational factors, one's belief about why people behave the way they do and what action can affect the problem is critical. Confidence also translates into an eagerness to become involved in genuine professional development.

Desire to Succeed. The tension created by a drive to succeed can result in the need to accomplish the tasks given, to bring about timely referrals and monitor follow-up, to develop accurate assessments and treatment plans, to generate positive professional relationships with community social service agencies, and to develop the reputation of a problem-solver — both internally in the center and externally with other organizations.

Image Building. The social worker must become comfortable with marketing his/her skills and abilities, both internally and externally. This process must involve conscious action to demonstrate the need for social work — that is, the outcome of social work interaction in enhancing patient care — and the potential education enhancement the social worker can provide to other medical professionals on the staff.

Interpersonal Skills. The age-old question of administrators is "can they get along with other staff?" Being trained in human behavior and even extended work history in social work or related human service fields do not guarantee that a candidate will be able to get along with other staff. This skill is especially critical for social workers functioning in primary care settings. The best way to test this would be to direct a portion of the interview to assess the level of insight and methods of personal change and by detailed questioning of references about a candidate's relationship skills and his/her interprofessional training.

The preparation for medical social work is the same as for the other fields of social work. Many colleges offer a bachelor of arts with a major in social work. This usually includes as many as 35 hours in social work or related fields such as psychology, sociology, or anthropology and a practicum during the last year of the program.

There is also a master's degree from an accredited graduate school of social work, referred to as the M.S.W. This degree usually includes 55-60 graduate level hours in social work and related fields and a practicum of approximately one and one-half years. Currently, graduate schools of social work give preference to applicants who, after having attained a B.A. degree, have worked at least several years in the field. However, M.S.W. programs generally admit candidates who do not have a B.A. in social work. The M.S.W. is usually the degree necessary to advance in the professional field and to hold administrative positions. A primary care center should attempt to recruit and hire the M.S.W., for the following reasons.

1. Joint Commission on Accreditation of Health Care Organizations (JCAHO) directs that the plan chosen for providing social work services shall provide for administrative accountability and direction by an M.S.W. or a B.A. with an M.S.W. as a consultant (National Association of Social Work Policy Statements, 1975). The JCAHO therefore places formal responsibility in the hands of an M.S.W.

2. Providers in the primary care setting expect a professionally run social work department, similar to what they were exposed to during their training within tertiary hospital-based settings.

3. The problems presented at most primary care centers are complex. The social worker will need refined diagnostic and therapeutic skills in order to solve patient problems and to facilitate linkage with community agencies.

It is difficult to develop the skills and personality traits listed above without at least three years experience in a health care setting. Although financial pressures within the center and market may be geared toward recruiting new graduates, the administrator generally should not move in that direction unless the new graduate has a strong work history in human services or medicine.

Work experience in areas of mental health/psychiatry, substance abuse, family treatment, and program development are also desirable work histories. The varied work experience is important to prepare workers to be able to shift from assessing the psychiatric needs of patients to developing health promotion/disease prevention programs. Figure 10.1 lists suggested methods of rating candidates.

The Job Description. The job description should be constructed through collaboration of the chief clinical staff, administrator, and social worker after that person has been on the job for 30-60 days. The

Education	Points
Medical Social Worker with Training in Program Planning/Development	4
Medical Social Worker	3
MA Counseling (noneducational focus)	2
MA Counseling (educational focus)	1

Work History

Psychotherapy	
1-3 years	2
4 years or more	3
Counseling	
1-3 years	1
4 years or more	2
Alcoholism Treatment	1
Human Service Agency	1
Institutional Treatment	1
Program Planning & Development	
1-3 years	2
4 years or more	3
Medical Organization	
1-3 years	2
4 years or more	3

References

Conceptual Skills Above Average	3
Independent Work Habits (desire to succeed)	3
Positive Interpersonal Skills	2
Positive Management Relationships	2
Positive Personal Adjustment	2

Miscellaneous

Protected Class (other than sex)	3
Male (because of our low ratio of male/female staff)	2
Female	1

Interview	0-5

Figure 10.1 Medical Social Worker Selection Criteria

social worker should not be allowed to design his/her own job description around his/her interests or skills.

Evaluation. The evaluation process should take place during the first year, after three, six, and twelve months, comparing expected results with actual results. The evaluation should be two-fold: First, the posi-

POSITION: Medical Social Worker

POSITION DESCRIPTION: The Medical Social Worker is to provide general medical social work services to the center's patient population, facilitate communication between patients and staff, establish and/or facilitate cooperation between the center and community at large.

RESPONSIBLE TO: Clinical Services Coordinator

RESPONSIBILITIES:

Primary Responsibilities

1. Provide supportive service to patients (directly or by referral), including but not limited to the following areas: Financial aid, psychiatric consultation and treatment employment, vocational training, school adjustment, family counseling, substance abuse, crisis management, services to special groups such as the elderly, adolescents, veterans, and physically and mentally disabled.
2. Invite staff from community agencies to conduct workshops at the center that would be beneficial to patients. A specific example would be workshops that provide material information concerning career advancement.
3. Provide individual and group counseling to patients in need of this service.
4. Act as an advocate or consultant to patients who encounter difficulty in receiving services from private or public agencies or firms. This service would include: Written communication, completion of appeal forms, contacting governing boards or commissions, obtaining legal services, or contacting regulatory agencies.
5. Identify barriers to effective patient/staff communication.
6. Enable the staff to interpret more accurately patient behavior, with specific emphasis on the stresses of physical and/or mental illness.
7. Increase staff awareness of the influence of cultural and socioeconomic factors on patient response to diagnosis and treatment.
8. Disseminate information on services available at the center.
9. Increase public awareness of the importance of continuing health care.
10. Encourage public involvement in the eradication of universal health problems such as substance abuse, social diseases, etc. One method of accomplishing this would be through workshops cooperatively planned and implemented with other community agencies, organizations, or institutions.
11. Other duties delegated by Clinical Services Coordinator or Project Director.

General Responsibilities

1. Actively and positively participate in staff meetings.
2. Work with supervisor to find solutions and resolve work-related problems, including equipment, procedures, peer relationships, and management directives.
3. Maintain work area in clean and orderly manner.
4. Strive for meeting organizational as well as personal goals.

POSITION REQUIREMENTS:

— Require M.S.W.
— Three (3) years experience in human service agency.
— Skills in problem solving, individual and group counseling; ability to relate effectively with patients in crisis.

Figure 10.2 Position Description

tion should be evaluated to determine if it accomplishes the goals of the setting; and second, the individual should be evaluated to determine if he/she is performing in a competent, professional manner (see Figure 10.2, Position Description).

The administrator must be available and knowledgeable if such an evaluation is to be useful. The development of a viable social work department is not an easy task but is one that can be accomplished through a cooperative effort.

CONCLUSION

Inappropriate and unrealistic expectations are the major problems facing social workers and administrators in the primary care setting. The administrator can alleviate this problem through good management. If the processes described in this chapter are followed, misunderstanding will be kept to a minimum and all energies can be devoted to solving patient problems.

REFERENCES

Bracht, N. (1977). *Basic premises underlying social work practice and planning in health services*. Paper presented at the 1977 meeting of the Society for Hospital Social Work Directors of the American Hospital Association, New Orleans.

Hirsch, S., & Lurie, A. (1969, April). Social work dimensions in shaping medical care philosophy and practice. *Social Work*.

Chapter 11

THE PHYSICIAN'S PERSPECTIVE

Paul M. Fischer

INTRODUCTION

Most physicians have little formal education regarding the variety of services that social workers can provide in the medical environment. The physician's experience comes principally through informal contact with social workers while providing care to hospitalized patients. This chapter begins with vignettes from my personal introduction to social work. I think these are typical for most other primary care physicians. These vignettes highlight not only the misconceptions that physicians have toward social workers but also the patient care benefits that can result when social workers and physicians collaborate effectively. The chapter also discusses interprofessional collaboration and the roles social workers can play in a changing health care environment.

PHYSICIAN TRAINING EXPOSURE TO SOCIAL WORK

In the summer after my first year of medical school, I participated in a family medicine preceptorship, part of which was spent in the office of a family physician. The remainder of the time was designated as "community medicine." This is an ambiguous term encompassing the many factors that affect health but are not directly under the physician's influence. I learned that the "community" is where most of the determinants of health existed and also where many nonphysician health care professionals worked.

The community medicine portion of the preceptorship had been designed to provide balance and perspective to my training. As part of this program, I spent time with a pharmacist, a minister, and a visiting nurse. My next experience was at a mental health clinic where I was to meet an "MSW." "What is an MSW?" I wondered.

The mental health clinic was a large, old Victorian building that needed restoration. I sat in the waiting area while the social worker was with a patient. I wondered what the two were doing. Eventually a tearful young woman came out, followed by the social worker. They scheduled a follow-up appointment, then the social worker invited me into his office. I asked him about his work. He told me that he saw patients for most of the day and that each encounter lasted about one hour. Most of what he did was counseling. His patients suffered from depression, anxiety, or character disorders. I remember thinking to myself, "How can he be doing counseling? Isn't that what psychiatrists do?" This affected my preconceived ideas about the physician's special role in society. I wondered if the AMA knew that this sort of thing was going on.

I had little contact with social workers during the first three years of medical school. Most of my clinical training occurred in academic hospital environments. In these settings, your interactions with other people are largely determined by your place in the "pecking order." Attending physicians talk to other attending physicians. Senior residents talk to junior residents. Junior residents talk to interns. Interns talk to nurses, physical therapists and social workers. Students talk to clerks in the lab, clerks in the radiology file room, and to patients.

It was not until my internship year that I learned more about social workers and their roles in the care of patients. The principal measure of an intern's skills is how few patients he or she "has." Admissions are usually distributed equally among interns. There are four eventual patient outcomes: the patient gets better and is discharged; the patient dies; the patient is transferred to another suitable service (i.e., a "turf"); or the patient enters a nursing home. The star intern has the fewest patients because of his/her ability to expedite these outcomes. The most troubling of the four outcomes for the intern is arranging nursing home placement. I learned that this is one of the principal roles for a hospital based social worker. It was called "discharge planning."

From my survivalist view as an intern, I placed social workers in two categories. Some were helpful and some were not. The helpful social

worker was able to "place" a patient in two to three days. It might take
a little longer if the patient had bed sores or incontinence, or was
"known throughout the system." A very helpful social worker was even
able to "hold the bed" in a nursing home for a few days while a patient
with chronic lung disease was "tuned up" in the hospital. According to
the intern gossip, some social workers had been known even to walk on
water.

But a social worker could also be an intern's nemesis. These social
workers never knew where the available nursing home beds were. They
might even be unable to arrange transportation home for a patient who
was ready for discharge. To a stressed intern, these shortcomings rep-
resented cruel and unusual punishment.

It is unfortunate that much of the early contact between physicians
and social workers occurs during the physician's year of internship.
These experiences can lead to unfortunate attitudes that influence a
physician's later practice. To the intern, a social worker's role is one-
dimensional: that is, the control of nursing home beds. Communication
between the intern and the social worker is often limited to orders in a
patient's chart, cryptic notes, and messages relayed over the beeper
system. The social worker is responsible for the forms that appear in
the front of the patient's chart and that the intern is responsible for
filling out. Often a social worker is the bearer of the bad news that a
patient does not qualify for a nursing home bed. The social worker
therefore may come to represent the injustice and illogical bureaucracy
that prevents the discharge of patients who no longer benefit from
hospital care.

After the completion of my residency I moved to the rural Midwest
and started a solo practice. In that unlikely spot away from the tertiary
hospital environment, I met a different type of social worker. I learned
a great deal from him about the potential role of social workers in the
primary care setting. We became friends and colleagues.

This social worker was the administrator of the county mental health
agency. That in and of itself was a challenge because the county was
primarily settled by proud Midwestern farmers. If you were to ask them
about the county's mental health problems, they would tell you they
had none. Mental health problems had never existed and probably
never would. There were, however, many ulcers if the rains came too
early or too late. There was a great deal of insomnia when the crop
prices fell. Families lost their farms from bank foreclosures. But there
were no mental health problems. They just did not believe in that sort
of thing.

The first thing that I noticed was that the mental health administrator did not limit his activities to following physician orders or to caring for the few patients seen in counseling sessions. Instead, he felt responsible for the entire community's mental health. He identified current problems in the community and worked to prevent potential ones. He worked with the local school board and the PTA to initiate sex education classes in the schools. He organized a group of community leaders to address problems with drug abuse in the schools and the rising rates of alcohol-related automobile accidents. He started a therapy group for elderly women who suffered from social isolation. He referred to all these activities as "outreach" and complained that the state administrators discouraged these activities by tying the clinic's reimbursement solely to the number of one-on-one patient counseling sessions. I was intrigued by his sense of responsibility for the entire community and modeled my own role on it.

The second unique quality about this social worker was that he related to me as an equal. He did not see himself as a subservient "allied health" practitioner. He treated me with respect and expected me to treat him in the same way. I had expected this type of relationship with other physicians but not with social workers.

Patients with mental health problems benefited from our collaboration. I would identify a patient in my practice who might benefit from counseling and would give him a call. He would identify a patient from his practice who might benefit from pharmacologic therapy and would give me a call. We talked weekly about each patient's case and their responses to therapy. Our communication was apparent to patients, and they greatly appreciated such coordination of care.

FACILITATING COLLABORATION

As can be seen from the vignettes, my thoughts about social work have changed over time. Regarding the role of a social worker, I went from misconception to a restricted view and finally to a fuller understanding of the potential role in a health care setting. In terms of interprofessional relationship, I changed my way of relating from hierarchical to collaborative. My care for patients shifted from working with social workers in a very narrow, task-defined way, to working with them as my consultants. Consultation is a time-honored tradition in medicine. Consultation occurs between equals with different types of expertise.

These shifts in my thinking were due largely to the unique individuals with whom I worked. The experience may not therefore be shared generally by other physicians. Mechanisms are needed, therefore, to facilitate better interprofessional collaboration. I offer three mechanisms, but many other approaches are possible.

Interprofessional training. Medical students in their preclinical years should be introduced formally to social work. At the Medical College of Georgia, this is done during their community medicine course. Students are divided into small groups of four or five. Each small group is given a one-page description of a hypothetical patient with several social problems. A typical example is an elderly patient with a recent stroke who has a dense hemiparesis; the patient has no family support and limited funding. Each group is also assigned a social worker in one of the local hospitals, with whom they meet to discuss the case. The medical students are then sent into the community to talk with agencies which provide community resources, such as Alcoholics Anonymous, Health Department, and Medicaid. Each group then writes a "solution" to the patient's problem. This exercise puts medical students into the learner role with social workers as teachers. It also sensitizes students to nonbiological aspects of health care and to community resources that are available to help solve patients' social problems.

Social workers and medical students need opportunities to interact during their clinical training. The most convenient setting for this to occur is during "attending rounds." These are didactic sessions organized by attending physicians that occur three to five times a week. Typically they last for two hours. The attending physician teaches the medical students and residents from the patient care problems that are currently on the teaching service. This is a good occasion for the social worker to teach, to model collaborative relationships with physicians, and to review the social work needs of the patients on the service.

Shared medical records. In most medical records, there is a separate section specifically for the physician's notations. All other individuals involved in the patient's case write in another portion of the chart. With this practice, the physician can easily overlook data important to a patient's care. Some hospitals are shifting from this traditional method, particularly in regard to nursing notes. This is obviously a sensible change and should be extended to social workers and other health professionals involved in patient care.

Social work rounds. Less than optimal communication will continue among social workers and physicians as long as their communication is limited to the "physician orders" section of hospital charts. What is needed are opportunities for physicians and social workers to meet face-to-face to discuss the care of patients. There are many examples of this type of interaction with other health professionals. The most common is the shared rounds by a physician and the charge nurse. The same type of rounds with a physician and social worker could improve the level of interprofessional communication. The new pressure for early discharge from the hospital has made the need for this sort of improved communication even more acute.

CHANGES IN HEALTH CARE AND THEIR EFFECTS ON SOCIAL WORK

Medicine is undergoing a revolution. The two most significant changes are the reorganization of the delivery of health care services and the recognition of the limits of medical technology. These are both fortuitous changes for social workers who are looking to expand their professional roles.

Medicine has seen a dramatic change in the way health care is delivered. Fewer physicians are in solo practice and less medical care is being paid for on a fee-for-service basis. Instead, physicians either are taking salaried positions at health care organizations or are working on a prepaid contractual basis. This shift is likely to continue.

Modern medical care is "managed." This means that the groups who are paying for care have a better understanding of what the care costs and what the true benefits to treatment are. In managed-care systems, the health professional who can provide the least expensive care while maintaining quality services will be favored. This has had the effect of blurring some of the rigid professional roles that were based principally on tradition. If a nonphysician provides quality service at a more competitive price, managed-care likely will seek that person's services.

The second important change has been the recognition of the limits of medical technology. This awareness is a result of spending large sums of money on sophisticated technology and finding that in many cases it did little to improve either the quality or length of people's lives. Such experience brought three major changes to the practice of medicine. First has been the willingness of health care professionals to examine more openly issues of quality of life rather than just quantity of life. Hospice is an example of this change in relating to terminally ill patients. Second, it has led to a new emphasis on health promotion and disease prevention. Physicians are now balancing the expensive, high-tech care that patients receive at the end of life with earlier efforts to prevent disease. Third, the acceptance of the limits of technology has led to a wider respect for the psychosocial view of illness. There is a renewed interest in the "art" of medicine and a recognition that it is just as important to know the person with the disease as to know the disease the person has.

In a broad sense, then, the changes in health care revolve around issues of organization and nonprocedural-oriented care issues that are fundamental also to social work. It is therefore an opportune time for social workers to expand their health care roles. But expansion will be possible only if social workers change their own perceptions of their roles. The medical social worker has been traditionally affiliated with hospitals, with physicians' "orders," and with "finding beds."

> Doctors have valued the social worker's capacity to identify, liaise with and coordinate appropriate services outside the health care organization, particularly when this facilitated the effectiveness of their own treatment or made possible more rapid discharge of patients from hospital beds. Social workers have never denied the importance of this function. Performed well, it eases the transition of patients through various stages of their condition and various types of care. They have, however, resented their confinement to this function by more dominant health officials. (Huntington, 1986, p. 1151)

What positions will social workers play in the new health care environment? I suggest four.

Patient counselor or therapist. Primary care physicians and social workers can collaborate positively with the social worker providing mental health counseling. Most primary care physicians routinely provide some psychological therapy. Few are trained or have time, however, to provide the intensive counseling that some patients require. In this situation, the physician usually identifies the person needing counseling and refers that person to a social worker. A social worker provides the majority of the counseling while the physician continues to provide other medical services. Physicians often can reinforce the care provided by the social worker and prescribe useful medications. The most common conditions that would be referred by a primary care physician to a social work counselor include anxiety, depression, characterologic disorders, somatiform disorders, and family adjustment problems. The increased attention to the behavioral aspects of medicine in physician training should lead to more efficient case identification by physicians as part of routine patient care. It is, however, very unlikely that it will lead to many primary care physicians spending one hour, once or twice a week, with individual patients to provide intensive counseling. Physicians and social workers therefore can continue to have complementary roles rather than competitive ones.

Health promotion/disease prevention. With the renewed attention to life-style-related disorders, an increased emphasis emerges on patient education and the development of health promotion/disease prevention programs for high-risk patients. To meet this need, social workers have to develop skills in public health, outreach and patient education. The traditional areas for patient education have been related to obesity, tobacco use, drug compliance, alcohol abuse, and sexuality. Each of these can have major public health consequences. Many other more narrowly focused areas of patient education, such as AIDS education, are also possible.

Health care administration. Decision-making within health care systems has shifted from physicians toward new health care administrators. These people come from a variety of backgrounds, such as business, social work, and public health. Opportunities for health care administration include the government, HMOs, PPOs, hospitals, and group practices. Health care administration is a rapidly growing field and one to which social workers are well-suited because of their experience in identifying resources to solve problems. The successful administrator in a health care setting can identify problems, analyze the cost for health care services, and document the effect of these services on patients' health. The cost of care and the quality of care are the two key aspects of the managed-care industry.

Community resource coordinator or social advocate. Although social workers traditionally have filled the role of social advocate, their services usually have been limited to meeting the needs of hospitalized patients. This was fine as long as most of the patients needing social work services were in the hospital and as long as there was little pressure to rapidly discharge patients in hospital beds. Even if patients are not sick enough to require hospitalization, they require the same help with locating community resources. Unfortunately, too few systems are available to either physicians or patients who wish to take advantage of social worker resources outside of the hospital. The shift from inpatient to outpatient care should lead to the development of more social work services in the primary care outpatient setting. The emphasis here will be less on finding nursing home beds and more on linking patients with community resources.

The ability of social workers to meet the needs of this changing health care system will depend on their resourcefulness and their ability to adapt to this new setting. I think four qualities will be essential.

First, social workers must be open to a shift in the "world-view" of their roles. They no longer will be based primarily in hospitals and their roles will not be limited to identifying empty nursing home beds. Physicians may not serve as their primary referral base. Social work education will need to change to incorporate more of a problem-solving approach and more field work in primary care settings.

Second, social workers will need to initiate services rather than wait for referrals. This is true especially for the identification of new problems that are amenable to social work solutions. Physicians no longer will determine what is an "appropriate" social work problem. Instead, the social worker will need to identify problems within the community or the health care system and then serve as a troubleshooter to bring the appropriate resources to bear on that problem.

Third, social workers will need to accept some ambiguity in their roles. This is true especially in terms of the territoriality of physicians. It is likely that the physician's and social worker's roles will overlap at times. Social workers must recognize that physicians' training often results in their assuming leadership even when faced with uncertainty. When this occurs, a defensive posture is less useful than a collegial one, which permits both the physician and social worker to identify how they can work together to solve a problem.

Fourth, social workers will need to look for new sources of income. It is unlikely that physicians in private practices will hire full-time social workers. In addition, the opportunities for social work "private practice" will decrease as managed and prepaid care becomes more common. The principal employers of social workers in the future are likely to be organizations that manage health care. Some of these will be government organizations but most will be part of the private health care industry.

People resist change. In the past, physicians have actively resisted the inevitable changes in the American health care system. The remarkable thing is how well most physicians have adapted. The current movement in health care toward primary care provides social workers with an ideal opportunity to reshape their own professional roles and to have a positive effect on the public's health.

REFERENCE

Huntington, J. (1986). The proper contribution of social workers in health practice. *Social Science Medicine, 22*, 1151-1160.

Chapter 12

FUTURE TRENDS OF SOCIAL WORK IN PRIMARY CARE

Christine L. Young

This chapter describes trends in public and private primary care settings and discusses selected health care issues that will affect the future role of social workers. Primary care will continue to be an essential and expanding component of the health care delivery system. This is evident in the many hospitals offering primary care to establish new profit centers and to ensure a steady source of patients who will use their facilities for inpatient and subspecialty outpatient care.

Other indicators include 1) continued federal support for community health and migrant health centers, the maternal and child health and children and youth projects, and family medicine residency programs; 2) the continuation of the health maintenance (HMO) programs including prepayment and capitalization under the Medicaid program; 3) the continued trend of physicians in group medical practices rather than in solo practices; and 4) the movement of city and county health departments to integrate and expand categorical services into primary care models.

The American Academy of Family Practitioners recently reemphasized the fact that there is and will continue to be a shortage of family physicians and other primary care specialists. Thus, the 300 existing family practice residency programs that function also as group practices will continue to be needed to train these primary care physicians and to serve patients.

Social work professionals can expand the scope and quality of care provided in these settings if we develop the skills necessary to assist patients, physicians, and administrators.

PUBLICLY FUNDED PRIMARY CARE SETTINGS

Federal. Approximately 550 federally funded community and migrant health centers exist in the United States (Sections 330 and 340 of the Public Health Service Act, 94:63). These centers serve over five million users, many of whom have low incomes and significant psychosocial problems. Although the psychosocial aspects of health care services, including the role of social work services, were emphasized during the early years of these programs, their necessary administrative and fiscal support was not always provided (Geiger, 1984). Because social work services in these programs have been limited and difficult to measure, the United States Public Health Service Region VII (Chicago) conducted a survey in 1985-1986 to determine the extent of social work involvement. The survey of administrators of 63 programs in Illinois, Indiana, Iowa, Wisconsin, Ohio, and Minnesota showed that:

1. Social services (e.g., counseling, referrals) often were provided by other personnel such as nurses and physicians.
2. Social services often were equated with mental health services, especially in programs with contractual arrangements with community mental health centers.
3. Administrators were hesitant to apply for funding for social work positions because continued federal funding was not assured for more than 1-3 years.
4. Administrators were aware of the value of social work but few were willing to commit scarce grant dollars to pay for it.
5. Primary care projects seldom had organized plans to address patient needs for social services and often relied on nurses to refer patients to community agencies.
6. There was little support from external sources to develop better social work services because they are not reimbursable services.

Although the results of this survey showed a general decline in traditional methods of funding social work positions in federally funded primary care programs, two important favorable findings emerged. First, the majority of the administrators recognized the value of social work services. Second, administrators recognized the extent and severity of social problems within their patient populations and the potential effect those problems could have on patient usage and the fiscal health of their programs. It is likely that with continued funding of these programs, additional social work positions may be created. The recent 19-million dollar supplemental grants to provide case management services for perinatal patients is one example of the way funds will be allocated.

Several other recent developments in federally funded primary care programs will affect the status of social work in these programs. First, there is a movement to provide social work services for "special populations." Such groups include high-risk maternal and child health populations — especially during the perinatal period — the homeless, children with AIDS, and persons with problems with substance abuse.

These groups have multiple social and health problems that demand multidisciplinary and case management approaches to their health care. With greater focus on special populations, social workers may refine their specialty practice. Gerontological social work in primary care is one example of a specialty area. This trend is evident in the present practice of hospital-based social workers who often work full-time in specialty services such as neonatology, obstetrics, and gynecology. The social work specialist has a greater capacity to acquire in-depth knowledge and skills related to a particular population group and to become an integral member of the professional community that addresses a certain disease or condition. As social workers understand how to intervene earlier in the disease process, their role should evolve from one of crisis intervention with tertiary problems to a public health approach focused on primary prevention for high-risk populations within primary care settings (Hall & Young, 1982; Kumabe, Nishida, O'Hara, & Woodruff, 1977).

Second, social workers must be able to record and document the screening, diagnosis, treatment, and outcomes that relate to their delivery of service. New federal guidelines stress the need to identify changes in patients' health that result from interventions. It is essential that social workers collect data demonstrating the quantity and quality of their contributions to the health services for specific individuals, patient populations, and for the primary care program as a whole.

Although little is written about city and county operated primary care programs, these programs are widespread and usually have a social work component. Most local health department clinics offer services such as maternal and child health, family planning, children and young, well child clinics, and women's, infants', and children's nutritional services. Unfortunately, these clinics usually do not provide organized, comprehensive primary care services, in part because they do not want to compete with private practitioners. As trends in Medicaid limit reimbursement for low-income and Medicaid patients, private practitioners likely will locate outside the inner city. If this happens, primary care programs subsidized by states and counties will be necessary. Because these programs serve high-need population groups, they probably will expand their services to include a variety of roles for social workers.

Finally, increasing and retaining the patient population will become a financial imperative for all health service programs. A well-developed social work program can increase users and encounters. This could be accomplished by developing health promotion/disease prevention programs, improving the comprehensiveness of care, reducing the dropout and absentee rates, and identifying new patient populations in need of primary care services (Rehr, 1984).

PRIVATE SECTOR PRIMARY CARE SETTINGS

Despite concern over the relatively high proportion of psychosocial and mental health problems physicians encounter during the delivery of primary health care (Hankin, Steinwachs, & Regier, 1982; Kessler, Burns, & Shapiro, 1987), social work has had little involvement in the private sector of primary care in the United States (Green & Kruse, 1985; Hookey, 1978). Social work services in primary care settings are relatively common in the Netherlands, Great Britain, and Australia (Corney, 1983; Huygen, 1962). The primary health care system in the United States is more individualistic and competitive than is the socialist primary care program in Great Britain.

It was expected that the United States' HMO movement, which includes over 1,000 programs, would generate a new work setting for social workers in primary care. Unfortunately, the HMO system has not met expectations for revenue or growth, and many HMOs are plagued by financial problems (Lum, 1976; Mayer & Rubin, 1983).

Despite such problems, many employers hope that the HMO system will stabilize the cost of health care plans for their employees. To increase their effectiveness in this area, HMOs may need to develop health promotion and disease prevention programs at employment sites. Social workers should prepare themselves for a public health role because such positions likely will be available in the future.

Other new opportunities for social work will occur, as hospitals expand their outpatient care programs and begin to locate them at geographically dispersed sites. Most hospital social work departments address the sickest patients or most complex situations, however. For this reason, hospital administrators may be reluctant to expand to these geographically dispersed primary care sites.

Historically, hospital social work departments have expanded by staffing specialty teams within the hospital. Often social work department directors have downplayed the role of generalist hospital social work because it has been easier to win financial and political support for a social work specialty position.

Discharge planning — another important aspect of social work — has gained significance because prospective payment systems and other review mechanisms have decreased the length of hospital stays. Because discharge planning has been a priority, developing and promoting new social work positions in geographically distant primary care settings has not occurred as quickly or completely as needed. Social work administrators must pursue new opportunities for hospital social workers in primary care settings while preserving the current social work functions within the inpatient programs.

The financial organization of health care is undergoing great change and with it comes increased accountability, greater emphasis on community-based care, and financial competition for patients among ambulatory and hospital practices. The changes will require additional support services, particularly case management services provided by professional social workers. One area of potential growth is private medical practice. The growth of multiphysician group practices creates an organizational structure and a patient workload large enough to justify the employment of social work professionals.

Two trends indicate that funding will become less of an issue for social work services in primary care. One is greater access to third-party reimbursement for social work services from private insurance plans in states with social work licensure. Another is public insurance plans for support services for selected groups such as high-risk perinatal populations.

Still other services could be developed by social work consultants or social workers in private practice. One category is social work services such as parenting skills, promotion of breastfeeding, or diabetes management, in collaboration with professionals such as nurses or nutritionists associated with the primary care site. Another area is referral/case management services used by physicians in gerontology practice with a high proportion of elderly needing home care, social services, counseling, or recreation referrals that promote good health. Social workers in private practice could also promote joint practice or a contractual arrangement with groups of physicians for counseling and similar services.

ISSUES IN PROFESSIONAL EDUCATION

Some authors have speculated that the lack of social work field placements in primary care has contributed to physician disinterest in employing social workers (Lowry, 1986). Although HMOs promised to be excellent settings for social work practice (Lum, 1976), they did not employ social workers to the extent originally anticipated (Mayer & Rubin, 1983).

Previous studies (Greene, Kruse, & Arthurs, 1985; Greene, Kruse, & Kupler, 1986; Gropper, 1987) show that family practice physicians are not inclined to use external counseling programs to treat patients with psychosocial problems or to employ social workers within the practice for these services. A recent survey of private primary care family physicians (Greene, Kruse, & Kupler, 1986) shows a lessening of that trend, however. According to Greene, Kruse, and Arthurs (1985), social workers might have the greatest opportunities for employment in these types of practices: 1) family physician treating fewer than 500 or more than 800 patients per month; 2) four or more physicians in group practices; 3) physicians 60 years old or younger who previously had family practice residencies; and 4) practices in urban communities.

Social work education has tended to focus its training and practicum sites within hospitals. As with medical education, the social work field placement sites have been in organizations that have had the greatest availability of professional social work supervision. Because primary care programs often do not employ professional social workers, or they are one-person social work departments, the base for social work training has been inadequate.

Social work in primary care has contributed significantly to maternal and child health programs (see, for example, Kumabe, Nishida, O'Hara, & Woodruff, 1977). The long-term federal commitment to social work training research and service within the Maternal and Child Health Program is an excellent example of the continuity of leadership and financial support available through Title V of the Social Security Act. The leadership of the federal Maternal and Child Health Program has provided faculty and student support for research, curriculum development, and continuing education. With additional financial support, this model may be extended to include greater social work involvement in primary care settings.

SELECTED TRENDS

Changes in reimbursement and coverage for uninsured individuals will greatly affect the future of primary care programs and social workers' involvement in them. Primary care settings are becoming larger and more systematized. If uninsured patients become eligible for health care coverage, they likely will be enrolled in large primary care programs to stabilize costs and to hold such programs accountable for quality care.

It is unlikely that reimbursement for uninsured patients will be met by an expanded Medicaid program in which reimbursement is essentially fee-for-service. Instead, the insurer, be it the federal or state government, will probably contract with a specific provider such as an HMO, group practice, or community health center to provide the service under a capitation program that establishes a set fee for each patient for each year of service. Public sector, city, and county primary care clinics will be asked to serve this group of patients. Regardless, it is likely that a comprehensive systematic primary care program will be needed to serve this population, and social workers will have a significant role in that effort.

Reimbursement for social work services in primary care includes fee-for-services, third-party reimbursement, and other financial arrangements such as waivers for social services to particular populations. Opportunities for reimbursement are most likely in states that have social work licensure, programs for the medically indigent, and special populations for whom providers receive payment for support services such as social work. Medicaid expansion, for example, may cover additional services, and preventive services such as social work may be added to Medicare and Medicaid benefits.

No single trend indicates a greater integration of social work into primary care. Many trends, however, indicate an awareness of the effect of psychosocial factors in health status, as well as changing attitudes toward the site of health care delivery, patient-provider relationships, and the role of patients in their own care. Recent government and private reports have related traditional programs such as Maternal and Child Health to the high rate of infant mortality (Brown, 1985; Institute of Medicine, 1985; Miller, 1985; National Commission to Prevent Infant Mortality, 1988); problems with financial access to prenatal care by large segments of the childbearing population (Gold, Kenney, & Singh, 1987); nonfinancial barriers to prenatal care (Curry, 1987); and access to pediatric care for medically neglected children (Butler, Winter, Singer, et al.,1985; Committee on Child Health Financing, American Academy of Pediatrics, 1987).

Self-help groups are becoming more important for several reasons: hospitals need to discharge patients as soon as possible; many hospitals regard self-help groups as potential sources of patient referrals and as agents for discharge planning; and primary care physicians and patients prefer in-home treatment, which requires support from self-help groups. Although self-help groups vary extensively in their inclusion of social workers and other professionals, social workers in health care participate/serve as volunteer facilitators or as facilitators at their workplaces (Black & Drachman, 1985; Madara & Neigher, 1986). Social work involvement to date has been either within hospital social work practice or as volunteer facilitators, but social workers could function also as liaisons, facilitators, or coordinators of self-help group activities for primary care patients.

The trend of treating the elderly and the physically and mentally impaired within their own homes or in a community setting will create more complex case management problems for primary health care. Given the concerns of malpractice and ethics of treatment, as well as the complex support services needed by high-risk populations, social workers may be a needed resource for many practicing physicians, particularly those who practice in care groups such as those for a large number of older patients.

There has been interest also in many areas of health promotion such as smoking cessation and weight control; although such programs are included in social work, they typically are offered by for-profit groups or voluntary agencies, such as the American Cancer Society, which specialize in a specific health problem. Health promotion programs may expand to physician-based care in hospitals if they are viewed as fiscally advantageous. If so, social workers and other professionals may be able to develop health promotion programs. Lack of funding for preventive care from insurance coverage has kept these programs small and limited in focus within the nonprofit health care system.

The new field of psychoimmunology offers potential for social work practice. The professional health care community and scientists who study the immune system are more aware of the potentially significant effect of personality, life events, or stress on the development, severity, or outcome of particular diseases (Dohrenwend & Dohrenwend, 1974; Jenkins, 1976; Kessler, Burns, & Shapiro, 1987; Kissen, 1963; Horne & Picard, 1979). Early identification of patients at risk for the development of particular diseases, and the inclusion of social work clinical services for those who have been diagnosed could be important preventive health activities within primary care practice. Moreover, social workers could assist patients whose coping styles and reactions to stressful events may lead to further deterioration of their health (Cohen, 1981; Lazarus, 1970). Clinical social work services, case management of referrals to self-help groups, recreation, employment, and education are appropriate social work services in the field of psychoimmunology.

Another area for expanded social work activity is advocacy for populations using primary care services. In addition to established organizations such as the Children's Defense Fund, other agencies to which social work in primary care can contribute significantly are state associations for primary health care, established self-help groups, and grass-roots activities for newly identified primary health care problems. Advocacy, program evaluation, lobbying, and fund-raising all could benefit from the social worker's skills and experience in enhancing the quality of primary health care delivery systems (see Chapter 5).

CONCLUSION

In summary, social workers will have diverse opportunities in future primary care settings but no single pathway along that profession. Understanding each role in which social workers can function is essential if we intend to integrate successfully into the primary care setting. Social workers interested in careers in primary care should be active in seeking appropriate social work education and practicum experiences in community health settings; obtaining educational and work experience in the field of public health; and identifying a specialty area of primary care such as maternal and child health or gerontology for social work practice in a clinical, administrative, research, or advocacy position in primary health care.

Educational institutions that provide continuing education for social workers must continue and expand the opportunities for training for those who are interested in this type of practice experience. Finally, primary care settings have unlimited potential to solve human problems. The unique relationship that exists between the setting and the patient offers social workers an opportunity to intervene at all levels of the problem-solving process and to use all the experience and skill they possess.

REFERENCES

Abramson, J., & Mizrahi, T. (1986). Strategies for enhancing collaboration between social workers and physicians. *Social Work in Health Care, 12*, 1-21.

Black, R. B., & Drachman, D. (1985). Hospital social workers and self help groups. *Health and Social Work, 10*, 95-103.

Brown, S. (1985). Can low birthweight be prevented? *Family Planning Perspectives, 17*, 112-118.

Butler, J. A., Winter, J. D., Singer, J. D., et al. (1985). Medical care use and expenditure among children and youth in the United States: Analysis of a national probability sample. *Pediatrics, 76*, 495-507.

Cohen, F. (1981). Stress and bodily diseases. *Psychiatric Clinics of North America, 4*, 269-286.

Committee on Child Health Financing, American Academy of Pediatrics.(1987). Financing health care for the medically indigent child. *Pediatrics, 80*, 957-960.

Corney, R. H. (1983). The views of clients new to a general practice attachment scheme and to a local authority social work intake team. *Social Science Medicine, 17*, 1549-1558.

Curry, M. A. (1987). *Access to prenatal care: Key to preventing low birthweight*. Kansas City, MO: American Nurses' Association.

Dohrenwend, B. S., & Dohrenwend, B. P. (Eds.). (1974). *Stressful life events: Their nature and effects*. New York: John Wiley.

Geiger, H. J. (1984). Community health centers' health care as an instrument of social change. In V. Sidel & R. Sidel (Eds.), *Reforming medicine: Lessons of the last quarter century*, pp. 11-32. New York: Random House.

Gold, R., Kenney, A., & Singh, S. (1987). *Blessed events and the bottom line, financing maternity care in the United States*. New York: Alan Guttmacher Institute.

Greene, G., & Kruse, K. A. (1985). Social work in family practice: What are the prospects? *Social Work in Health Care, 11*, 89-97.

Greene, G., Kruse, K. A., & Arthurs, R. J. (1985). Family practice social work: A new area of specialization. *Social Work in Health Care, 10*, 53-73.

Greene, G., Kruse, K. A., & Kupler, T. (1986). Identifying potential family practice social work opportunities. *Social Work in Health Care, 11*, 89-97.

Gropper, M. (1987). A study of the preferences of family practitioners and other primary care physicians in treating patients' psychosocial problems. *Social Work in Health Care*, 75-92.

Hall, W. T., & Young, C. L. (1982). Social work in the field of public health. In D. Sanders, O. Kurren, & J. Fischer (Eds.), *Fundamentals of social work practice*, pp. 215-220. Belmont, CA: Wadsworth.

Hankin, J. R., Steinwachs, D., & Regier, D. A. (1982). Use of general medical services by persons with mental disorders. *Archives of General Psychiatry, 39*, 225-231.

Hookey, P. (1978). Social work in primary health care settings. In N. F. Bracht (Ed.), *Social work in health care: A guide to professional practice*, pp. 211-223. New York: Haworth.

Horne, R. L., & Picard, R. S. (1979). Psychosocial risk factors for lung cancer. *Psychosomatic Medicine, 41*, 503-514.

Huygen, F. J. A. (1962). Het home team. *Huisarts en Weteschap* [Netherlands], *5*, 119-123.

Institute of Medicine. (1985). *Preventing low birthweight*. Washington, DC: National Academy Press.

Jenkins, C. D. (1976). Recent evidence supporting psychologic and social risk factors for coronary disease. *New England Journal of Medicine, 294*, 987-994.

Kessler, L. G., Burns, B. J., & Shapiro, S. (1987). Psychiatric diagnosis of medical service users: Evidence from the epidemiological catchment area program. *American Journal of Public Health, 77*, 18-24.

Kissen, D. (1963). Personality characteristics in males conducive to lung cancer. *British Journal of Medical Psychology, 34*, 27-36.

Kumabe, K., Nishida, C., O'Hara, D., & Woodruff, C. (1977). *A handbook for social work education and practice in community health settings*. Honolulu: School of Social Work, University of Hawaii.

Lazarus, R. S. (1970). Cognitive and personality factors underlying stress and coping. In S. Levine & N. Scotch (Eds.), *Social stress*. Chicago: Aldine.

Lowry, C. F. (1986). Generic social work practice and family practice: Students build a foundation for partnership. *Social Work in Health Care, 12*, 15-25.

Lum, D. (1976). The social service health specialist in an HMO. *Health and Social Work, 1*, 29-50.

Madara, E. J., & Neigher, W. D. (1986). Hospitals and self-help groups: Opportunity and challenge. *Health Progress, 67*, 42-45.

Mayer, J. B., & Rubin, G. (1983). Is there a future for social work in HMOs? *Health and Social Work, 8*, 283-289.

Miller, C. A. (1985). Infant mortality in the United States. *Scientific American, 253*, 31-37.

National Commission to Prevent Infant Mortality. (1988). *Infant mortality: Care for our children, care for our future*. Washington, DC: Author.

Rehr, H. (1984). Health care and social work services: Present concerns and future directions. *Social Work in Health Care, 10*, 71-83.

AUTHOR INDEX

SUBJECT INDEX

acute care, 20
advocacy, 14, 28, 35, 37, 39, 46, 47, 50, 61, 62, 81, 86, 89-91, 179; case, definition of, 82, 88; class, definition of, 82, 92, 190; internal, definition of, 87; political, definition of, 88; resource development, definition of, 88
age/sex registry, 114, 120, 131, 140
AIDS, 8, 28, 39, 50, 87, 91, 115-117, 121, 179, 184
ambulatory care, 18; clinics, definition of, 13
American Academy of Family Practice, 11, 181
assessment, 57, 59, 60, 97, 106, 156
at risk, 42, 50, 52, 56, 70, 113, 114, 120, 190

brokerage, 14, 35, 46; definition of, 82; case management, 13, 27, 28, 67, 76, 87, 157, 184

casefinding, 37, 59, 70, 115
categorical services, 65, 113, 116, 164, 181
change, 62, 92, 119, 125, 145, 186
change agent, 35, 177
Children's Aid Society, 95
Children's Bureau, 21, 22, 24, 25
clinical rounds, 87, 176, 177
coach, 102, 109; definition of, 101
coalition, 60, 62, 90, 91, 117, 119
codes, 73, 129
cognitive map, 95, 99-101, 105
collaboration, 43, 48, 60, 82, 86, 94, 145, 146, 155, 172, 175, 176, 186
community health centers, 14, 15, 19, 22, 23, 33, 56, 181, 183, 188; definition of, 12
community organization, 37
compliance, 44, 47, 50, 59, 70, 106, 133, 135, 164

comprehensive care, 10, 12, 15, 20, 56, 69, 81, 94, 101, 108, 113, 148, 153, 161, 185
consortia, 119
consultant, 35, 155, 175, 186
consultation, 11, 14, 37, 51, 61, 91, 94, 95, 97, 99-102, 104-107, 109; definition of, 96
case, 107; definition of, 98
consumer, definition of, 110
continuity of care, 10, 11, 20, 44, 60, 101, 108, 113, 128
coordinated care, 11
Crippled Children's Service, 22
curriculum, 34, 43, 46, 48, 51, 52, 96, 188

data collection, 92, 97, 105, 106, 113, 114, 127, 130, 134
Diagnostic and Statistical Manual (DSM-III), 130
diagnostic index, 114, 130, 141

ecological systems, 37
enabler, 102, 109; definition of, 101
encounter form, 103, 138
entitlement programs, 83
epidemics, 19
epidemiology, 36, 38, 51, 57
episodic care, 11, 13
evaluation, 62, 74, 97, 100, 106, 114, 121, 169

facilitator, 102, 109; definition of, 101
family practice, 14, 15, 22, 23
family practice residency, definition of, 13
for-profit group, 14, 15, 120, 160
functions, 13, 157

generalist, 14, 35, 37, 55, 57, 61, 62
group practice, 19, 186, 188; definition of, 13, 182

ABOUT THE AUTHORS

ROBERT J. BATTJES (D.S.W., The Catholic University of America, 1982) is Associate Director for Planning, Division of Clinical Research, National Institute on Drug Abuse. He has edited several books and published articles on the etiology of drug abuse, drug abuse prevention, smoking, and the Acquired Immunodeficiency Syndrome. His current research is focused on AIDS-risk behaviors among intravenous drug abusers, and he is currently consulting with the Health Resources and Services Administration in the development of a demonstration program integrating primary care and specialty drug abuse treatment for intravenous drug abusers.

WILLIAM H. BUTTERFIELD (Ph.D., University of Michigan, 1970) is Associate Professor at the George Warren Brown School of Social Work, Washington University. He was principal coordinator for a National Institute of Mental Health Grant to evaluate behavioral interventions in rural primary care settings. He was also active in the training of family practice residents and medical students when he was Assistant Professor with the School of Social Work, University of Wisconsin (1970-1973).

JANE COLLINS (M.S.W., University of Denver, 1950) is Director of Clinical Social Work, Denver Department of Health and Hospitals. She developed the clinical social work components of the Community Health Center and Community Mental Health programs within Health and Hospitals. She wrote the social work guidelines for Maternity and Infant Care and Intensive Care for Newborns for the Title V of the Social Security Act Program of Projects. Publications have been focused on various aspects of maternal and child health and cost-effectiveness. She has had extensive experience developing training programs for and using para-professionals. She has developed revenue-enhancing programs which may be used by social workers in hospital and ambulatory settings. She was named Hospital Social Work Director of the Year in 1985 by the Society for Hospital Social Work Directors of the American Hospital Association. She is currently involved in two ambulatory projects—one concerning AIDS patients and the other focusing on continuity of care for low-income elderly.

LOUISE DOSS-MARTIN (M.A., University of Chicago, 1963) is Regional Public Health Social Work Consultant in the Chicago Regional Office, Department of Health & Human Services, serving a six-state region in the U.S. Public Health Service. She has had 16 years' clinical and administrative experience in the fields of mental health, maternal and child health, and primary care services, including positions as Director of Social Services in two major Community Health Centers in Chicago (1967-1971).

During her tenure in the Region V office (1976 to present), she has presented and published numerous papers and articles on topics related to minority health issues, and has recently coauthored the following research articles: "A Study of Factors Associated with Black Infant Mortality" (1985); "Black Infant Mortality: Historical and Current Perspectives" (1986); and "Black Maternal Mortality in Chicago, Detroit, and the U.S.: 1979-1984" (1987).

She is currently completing a 3-year project related to provision of social services in federally funded primary care projects in Region V, and has written two reports related to improvement of the quantity and quality of social services in primary care programs: "Findings of the Regionwide Survey on Provision of Social Services in Primary Care Projects—Region V" (1986), and *Guidelines for Developing Social Work Services in Primary Care Settings* (in press).

PAUL M. FISCHER (M.D., University of Connecticut, 1978) is Associate Professor in the School of Medicine, Medical College of Georgia. He was in solo practice in Weeping Water, Nebraska, prior to his move to the Medical College of Georgia. He currently serves as course director for a required second-year medical student course which includes an introduction to medical social work. This is done by having social workers lead small groups of medical students through simulated patient exercises. Dr. Fischer has written extensively in the areas of office laboratory testing and physician health promotion.

MATTHEW L. HENK (M.S.S.W., University of Wisconsin—Milwaukee, 1967) is the Public Health Social Work Consultant, U.S. Public Health Service, Kansas City, Missouri. He has developed numerous primary care group practices in underserved areas of Iowa, Nebraska, Kansas, and Missouri, and evaluates social work components in federally funded programs. He formerly taught Behavioral Sciences at the University of Rochester Family Practice Program (Clinical Associate Professor, 1973-77). During this time he convened a national meeting of social workers in family practice programs and coauthored an article in the *Journal of the American Medical Association* on outreach by primary care physicians (1975), and coauthored a chapter in the text *Family Practice* by Rankel, 1978. He has presented numerous papers at national meetings on topics related to social work in primary care. His interest is to improve primary health care delivery systems and to involve and assist social workers in this effort.

HOWARD J. HESS (D.S.W., University of Alabama, 1981) is Associate Professor and Assistant Dean of the Indiana University School of Social Work. His current academic responsibilities include teaching graduate-level coursework in the school's health concentration. He previously initiated an interdisciplinary training project for graduate social work students in the Department of Family Medicine at the University of Tennessee Center for the Health Sciences. His scholarly writing focuses upon the nature of biopsychosocial care in primary health care settings. In particular his work has examined the components of social work practice in family medicine and the emergency care setting, an area he most recently explored in the forthcoming volume *Crisis Intervention Sourcebook* (1990). He is currently engaged in several research projects related to the AIDS epidemic. These include a national study of the use of support groups for HIV+ persons and a study of the impact of AIDS upon the low impact state of Indiana. In addition he is the Client Services Chairperson of the Damien Center, an AIDS service organization in Indianapolis, Indiana, and the leader of a support group for HIV+ persons.

RONALD W. KEMP (M.S.W., University of Iowa, 1974) is Director of the People's Community Health Clinic in Waterloo, Iowa. He is a member of local, regional, and national associations of community health centers. He has directed the Health Center for ten years and has employed a variety of social workers to meet the mental health, public health, and social service needs of the clinic population.

CARL G. LEUKEFELD (D.S.W., Catholic University of America, 1975) is Chief Health Services Officer, U.S. Public Health Service and Deputy Director, Division of Clinical Research, National Institute on Drug Abuse. He is also an Adjunct Faculty Member, Virginia Commonwealth University. His seven coedited books include *Preventing Adolescent Drug Abuse: Intervention Strategies* and *Responding to AIDS: Psychosocial Initiatives* (1987). His current research involves the use of mandatory treatment for reducing HIV and drug abuse, financing of social services, and the effects of community prevention on changing health behaviors.

BETTY L. RUSNACK (M.S.W.,University of Michigan, 1946) is Emerita Professor, Wayne State University. During her tenure in the School of Social Work, she was active in planning and implementing interdisciplinary and primary care internships for nursing, medicine, pharmacy, social work, and other health professions. In her teaching and practice, she contributed to furthering the articulation of social work's concern for the social and emotional needs and problems of patients and families before, during, and after the onset of illness or disability. She presented numerous professional papers dealing with such themes as social work in family practice, continuity of health care, interdisciplinary education for health care, primary prevention and health promotion, and consumer participation. "Safe Passage: Social Work Roles and Functions in Hospice Care," *Social Work in Health Care* (1988), is representative of her current interests, which center on services for older citizens, Parkinson's support groups, home care, and the implementation of hospice concepts in health care.

KRISTINE SIEFERT (M.S.W., University of Michigan, 1975; M.P.H. and Ph.D., University of Minnesota, 1980) has had 15 years' experience as a practitioner, educator, and researcher in social work and public health. Currently Associate Professor of Social Work at the University of Michigan, she is co-coordinator of the M.S.W./M.P.H. dual degree program in social work and maternal and child health. She has served on Michigan's Statewide Task Force on Infant Mortality; on the Advisory Committee on Public Health Social Work for the Bureau of Health Care Delivery and Assistance, DHHS; and on the Council on Social Work Education Task Force on Primary Prevention. She has written extensively about social and behavioral factors in pregnancy outcome, on improving health care service delivery to underserved groups, and on primary prevention in health and mental health. She recently served as guest editor of a special issue of the *Journal of Primary Prevention* on prevention strategies in the problems of women.

DEBORAH J. STOKES (M.S.S.A., Case Western Reserve University, 1974) is a social work consultant for the Division of Maternal and Child Health, Ohio Department of Health. She has published on such topics as services for handicapped children, monitoring and evaluation, building social service networks, infant mortality, linking public health and public social services, and primary prevention of child abuse and neglect. Her current activities involve the development of primary prevention programs for the reduction of child abuse and neglect, and teenage pregnancy. In addition, she is responsible for directing the Governor's initiative on Parenting For Peaceful Families. Her major interests are in health and the Black family, Black infant mortality, AIDS, and adolescent health.

LANN E. THOMPSON has an Ed.D. in counseling psychology, an M.S.S.W. in social work, and an M.A. in educational psychology and counseling. He is currently Director of Social Work Training, and Outreach Training Coordinator at Riley Child Development Center, James Whitcomb Riley Hospital for Children, Indiana University Medical Center, Indianapolis, Indiana. He serves as an Adjunct Assistant Professor at the Indiana University School of Social Work, School of Nursing, and School of Medicine. He was coeditor for *Social Dimensions in the Delivery of Health Services* (1981) which focused on improving social work in primary care for the rural setting. His publications include numerous articles on social work in maternal and child health and children with special health care needs and their families. His latest work was development of a training curriculum on family-centered, community-based care coordination for primary care projects in maternal and child health. He is also the consultant for a model MCH project, Community Partners in Prenatal Care, which is developing public health nurse, social worker, community health worker teams to reduce infant mortality.

CHRISTINE L. YOUNG (M.S.W., 1972; M.Ph., 1977; Ph.D., University of Pittsburgh, 1979) is Assistant Professor of Community Health Services, Graduate School of Public Health, University of Pittsburgh. She received the A.C.S.W. in 1975. She recently served as a consultant to the Region V Office, U.S. Public Health Service, for a regionwide study of the provision of social services in primary care projects. In 1986, she completed a study of family planning and Black infant mortality for the Region III Office, U.S. Public Health Service. Her latest research and publications have focused on access to pediatric care, maternal reasons for delayed prenatal care, social services for very low birth weight infants, family planning utilization by minority women, health and human services for rural populations, and social work research methodology. She is a member of the Pennsylvania Forum for Primary Health Care and serves on the Advisory Board of the Allegheny County Alliance for Infants. In 1988, she was appointed to the Mayor's Commission on Families for the City of Pittsburgh.

NOTES

NOTES

NOTES

NOTES